Kingston Libraries

KT-548-211
UPON THAMES

EⁱⁱR

QUEEN ELIZABETH II

CROWNS, HORSES,

AND CORGIS

'Like all the best families, we have our share of eccentricities, of impetuous and wayward youngsters and of family disagreements.'

The Queen, quoted in the Daily Mail, October 1989

KINGSTON LIBRARIES

KT 2186528 0

Editor: Stephen Haynes
Editorial Assistants: Rob Walker, Mark Williams

Published in Great Britain in MMXVI by
Scribo, an imprint of
The Salariya Book Company Ltd
25 Marlborough Place, Brighton BN1 1UB
www.salariya.com
www.book-house.co.uk

HB ISBN-13: 978-1-910706-20-6

© The Salariya Book Company Ltd MMXVI

All rights reserved. No part of this publication may be reproduced,
stored in or introduced into a retrieval system or transmitted in any form,
or by any means (electronic, mechanical, photocopying, recording or
otherwise) without the written permission of the publisher. Any person
who does any unauthorised act in relation to this publication may be
liable to criminal prosecution and civil claims for damages.

3 5 7 9 8 6 4 2 1
A CIP catalogue record for this book is available
from the British Library.
Printed and bound in India.
Printed on paper from sustainable sources.

Photographic credits: p. 6, TopFoto.co.uk; p. 32, ©2003 Topham
Picturepoint/ TopFoto.co.uk; p. 64, © PA Photos/TopFoto.co.uk

This book is sold subject to the conditions that it shall not, by way of trade or otherwise, be lent,
resold, hired out, or otherwise circulated without the publisher's prior consent in any form or binding
or cover other than that in which it is published and without similar condition being imposed on the
subsequent purchaser.

Kingston upon Thames Libraries	
KT 2186528 0	
Askews & Holts	13-May-2016
JB/ELI	£6.99
TD	KT00001422

EₙR
QUEEN
ELIZABETH II

CROWNS, HORSES,

AND CORGIS

Written by

David Arscott

Created and designed by

David Salariya

SCRIBO

WORDS FROM THE THRONE

'I declare before you all that my whole life, whether it be long or short, shall be devoted to your service and the service of our great imperial family to which we all belong.'

The Queen on her 21st birthday, April 1947

'I cannot lead you into battle, I do not give you laws or administer justice but I can do something else: I can give you my heart and my devotion to these old islands and to all the peoples of our brotherhood of nations.'

Her first televised Christmas address, 1957

'When life seems hard, the courageous do not lie down and accept defeat; instead, they are all the more determined to struggle for a better future.'

Christmas address, 2008

Contents

HER MAJESTY
QUEEN ELIZABETH II
IN 1960

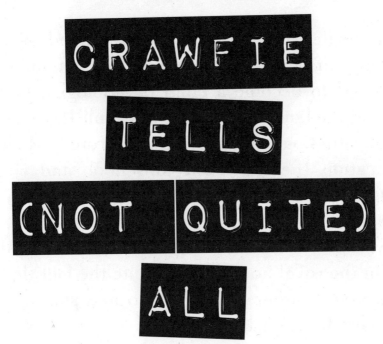

CRAWFIE TELLS (NOT QUITE) ALL

t was a major scandal which in our brasher and more muck-raking times now seems little more than a storm in a Royal Doulton teacup. In 1950 Marion Crawford, the beloved governess of the princesses 'Lilibet' and Margaret Rose, published an affectionate memoir which revealed innocent secrets of life with her young charges and their parents, George VI and Queen Elizabeth. Tame as these revelations were, 'Crawfie' was from that moment an outcast, and the inner circle of the royal family would never have her name mentioned in their hearing again.

The reviled Crawfie, who had trained as a teacher in her native Scotland and originally planned to become a child psychologist, had served the family devotedly for a full 16 years. After guiding the princesses through their education (neither went to school, and she taught them the Bible, arithmetic, history, geography, grammar, literature, poetry, music, drawing, writing and composition), she stayed on in the royal household despite the fact that she would rather have married and started a new life for herself.

CRAWFIE'S REVELATIONS I

The young princesses had constrasting personalities, with Margaret a more lively and wayward foil to her serious older sister. (Their father described Elizabeth as his pride and Margaret as his joy.)

While Margaret was a practical joker, a 'born comic', and could be disruptive, the dutiful Elizabeth always chose her words carefully and behaved with the utmost decorum.

And here's Elizabeth as moral guide: 'If you see someone with a funny hat, Margaret, you must not point at it and laugh.'

'You must see, Crawfie,' the Queen once told her dismissively, 'that it would not be at all convenient just now.'

In 1947, at the age of 40, she *did* at last marry, soon retiring to a 'grace and favour' cottage in the grounds of Kensington Palace and being made a Commander of the Royal Victorian Order by the King.

Her pay had never been great, though, and her pension was small – and in no time at all the American magazine *Ladies' Home Journal* came knocking on her door, tempting her with the then considerable fee of $85,000 to 'tell all' about her relationship with the future queen of England.

The articles she submitted to it (doctored by a ghost writer for public consumption) later appeared in *Woman's Own* magazine in Britain and were reproduced in book form, to great public interest, as *The Little Princesses*.

The Queen – soon to become the Queen Mother on the sudden death of George VI – had already warned Crawfie against putting her name to her reminiscences, telling her that 'People in positions of confidence with us must be utterly oyster.' In addition, she wrote sternly, 'You would lose all your friends, because such a thing has never been done or contemplated amongst the people who serve us so loyally.'

Now she was furious: 'We can only think that our late and completely trusted governess has gone off her head!'

Persona non grata

Question: What first brought Crawfie's disgrace home to her?
Answer: She wasn't sent her usual Christmas card by the royal family.

Worse was to follow:

• She was made to leave her grace and favour home.

• She and her husband bought a house in Aberdeen within sight of the royal family as they passed by on their way to Balmoral Castle – but none of them ever called in to see her.

- She put her name to the ghosted 'Crawfie's Column' in Women's Own, but in June 1955 this included 'reports' of Royal Ascot and Trooping the Colour, both of which had been cancelled because of a national rail strike. Her career as a royal columnist ended in ridicule.

- After her husband died, in 1977, she fell into depression, thinking of the old days, and attempted (unsuccessfully) to commit suicide.

- When she died in 1988 (her will poignantly leaving all her royal mementoes to Lilibet), the royals sent no wreath to her funeral.

CRAWFIE'S REVELATIONS 2

The young Elizabeth could be 'quick with her left hook', while Margaret was 'known to bite on occasions' when they squabbled.

When a French lesson became too taxing, Elizabeth once tipped an ornamental inkpot over her head, giving herself blue hair.

Princess Margaret 'looked like a little sausage' when wearing her bathing suit.

The princesses enjoyed pillow fights with their parents, and also liked to play hopscotch and hide-and-seek.

'MY SISTER AND I...'

Princess Elizabeth made her very first public broadcast on the BBC's **Children's Hour** radio programme on 13 October 1940, when she was 14 years old. With great composure, and with the distinctive upper-class vowels of her generation, she read a four-minute message to 'the children of the Empire', many of whom had been evacuated because of the war.

'All of us children who are still at home,' she said, 'think continually of our friends and relations who have gone overseas – who have travelled thousands of miles to find a wartime home and a kindly welcome in Canada, Australia, New Zealand, South Africa and the United States of America.'

'We know, every one of us, that in the end all will be well; for God will care for us and give us victory and peace. And when peace comes, remember it will be for us, the children of today, to make the world of tomorrow a better and happier place.'

The two sisters signed off together:

Elizabeth: 'My sister is by my side and we are going to say goodnight to you. Come on, Margaret.'

Margaret: 'Goodnight, children.'

Elizabeth: 'Goodnight, and good luck to you all.'

A QUEEN IN THE MAKING

What kind of a monarch did Crawfie's writings suggest that Elizabeth II would turn out to be?

• A conscientious late learner. George V, their grandfather, once barked at Crawfie: 'For goodness' sake, teach Margaret and Lilibet to write a decent hand – that's all I ask of you.' (In later life Margaret would complain about the poverty of their education.) Once she became heiress presumptive to the throne, however, Elizabeth was given a crash course in politics, current affairs and the history of the British constitution.

• Extremely orderly. Crawfie wrote that Elizabeth would obsessively 'stable' her 30 toy horses by her bed each night, and (hardly believable, surely) would jump out of bed several times a night to check that her clothes and shoes were still neatly arranged. Here are the two sisters eating barley sugar: 'Margaret kept the whole lot in her small, hot hand and pushed it into her mouth. Lilibet, however, carefully sorted hers out on the table, large and small pieces together, and then ate them daintily and methodically.'

• An outsider looking in. The princesses were fascinated by other children, according to Crawfie, and 'used to smile shyly at those they liked the look of. They would so have loved to speak to them and make friends, but this was never encouraged.' Elizabeth did become a girl guide, but at home, in the 1st Buckingham Palace Company – formed for her benefit in 1937 and packed with other well-to-do young girls. Nobody can doubt the Queen's kindly interest in her subjects, but she has always appeared a stranger on the plebeian shore.

IN THE LIMELIGHT

The royals would for ever afterwards refer to betrayals of confidence as 'doing a Crawfie', but the young Elizabeth – who came to the throne only two years after the publication of *The Little Princesses* – could never have imagined that the trickle of intimate detail in that first 'kiss and tell' story would soon become a turbulent and remorseless flood. The world had changed, and an insatiable media had begun to breach the dam of secrecy which had protected the royal family for generations.

One significant effect of the Second World War, as evidenced by the 'khaki election' which swept the Labour Party to power in its aftermath, was a new lack of deference to the old establishment – the Crown included.

A YOUNG SUBALTERN

As a girl Elizabeth was devoted to the hunting/ shooting pursuits of her class, being horse-mad and devoted to the family's corgis. During the war, however, she was determined to show her solidarity with the public at large by getting her hands dirty. She joined the Auxiliary Territorial Services (ATS) as subaltern no. 230873 – training as a mechanic and driving military vehicles.

Before that she had joined her parents on a series of national visits, and (at the age of 18) carried out the official duties of head of state while the King toured the Italian battlefields.

AN 'AUSTERITY' WEDDING

When Elizabeth married Philip, her Greek prince, in November 1947, the country was crippled by debt and still reeling from the deprivations of war. Philip was relatively skint and allegedly walked up the aisle in darned socks. (Changing his name and religion to hitch up with the Windsors must have seemed a good bargain.) It was billed as an 'austerity' wedding – the government awarded the Queen an extra 200 clothing coupons towards her outfit – but it would have suited many of Elizabeth's subjects very nicely, thank you.

The Archbishop of York told the 2,500 guests in Westminster Abbey that the ceremony was 'in all essentials exactly the same as it would have been for any cottager who might be married this afternoon in some small country church in a remote village in the Dales'. But there were six kings and seven queens in the congregation; Elizabeth arrived, fairytale-like, in a golden coach; and 350 girls had toiled for seven weeks to create her gown.

Once the ceremony was over, the happy couple rode in a glass coach to an austerity wedding breakfast for 150 people at Buckingham Palace. Their gifts ranged from the exotic to the humble (tins of rationed salmon and pineapple from an adoring public), while Mahatma Gandhi sent a hand-spun shawl which a shuddering Queen Mary (the Queen's grandmother) mistook for a loincloth.

Another effect of the war was a gradual loosening of strict social norms, such as the permanence of the marriage tie. Consider these cases:

- The young Elizabeth was destined to be Queen from the moment her uncle, Edward VIII, abdicated in 1936 to marry 'the woman I love'. The problem was that the woman he loved, Wallis Simpson, was a divorcee with two living ex-husbands and a racy lifestyle.

- In 1953, with Elizabeth about to be crowned, her sister Margaret requested permission to marry Group Captain Peter Townsend, a divorced father of two. The public generally approved of this love match, but in the end Margaret caved in to enormous pressure, 'mindful of the Church's teachings that Christian marriage is indissoluble, and conscious of my duty to the Commonwealth'.

- In 1967, Lord Harewood, the Queen's first cousin, was divorced by his wife for adultery. The royals had regularly visited Harewood House, near Harrogate, but now their kinsman was ostracised and they never went there again.

Alas, the comfortable notion that such dramas were exceptions to the rule was all too soon to be shattered – and very close to home, too.

The Queen herself would not only witness the divorces of her sister and three of her own four children, but would, metaphorically, watch a huge amount of their dirty linen being run up the Buckingham Palace flagpole. A royalty with feet of clay may appeal to those who would like the monarch to be 'one of us', but for millions the essential magic had gone. There were persistent calls for the creation of a republic.

The story that unfolds in these pages is therefore one of doughty determination – the story of a monarch who finds herself thrust into a new world of relentless public exposure, whose own family turns out to be as frail as everyone else's, but who yet somehow, for a full 63 years, manages to steer the institution through the choppy waters intact.

UP A FIG TREE

It was while on a royal visit to Kenya, in February 1952, that the 25-year-old Elizabeth learned that her father had died in the night. As the author William Shawcross put it, 'She is the only woman known to have gone up a tree a princess and come down a queen' – the explanation being that she and Prince Philip were staying at Treetops, a 'shack' built into a large fig tree on a game reserve.

She reacted with her customary composure, immediately flying home to tackle the daunting task before her. The drawbacks of her new existence were acknowledged a few days later in a speech by her mother, who now became the Queen Mother: 'I commend to you our dear daughter; give her your loyalty and devotion; in the great and lonely station to which she has been called she will need your protection and your love.'

In those seemingly now far distant days the nation did, as a whole, give the monarchy its love, and Coronation Day the following year was a splendid occasion, with street parties, bunting and the distribution of souvenir mugs.

Sixty-three years on, one 10-year-old who pasted newspaper cuttings into a Coronation scrap book to win third prize in a school competition finds himself compiling a rather different, more nuanced, account of the second Elizabethan age...

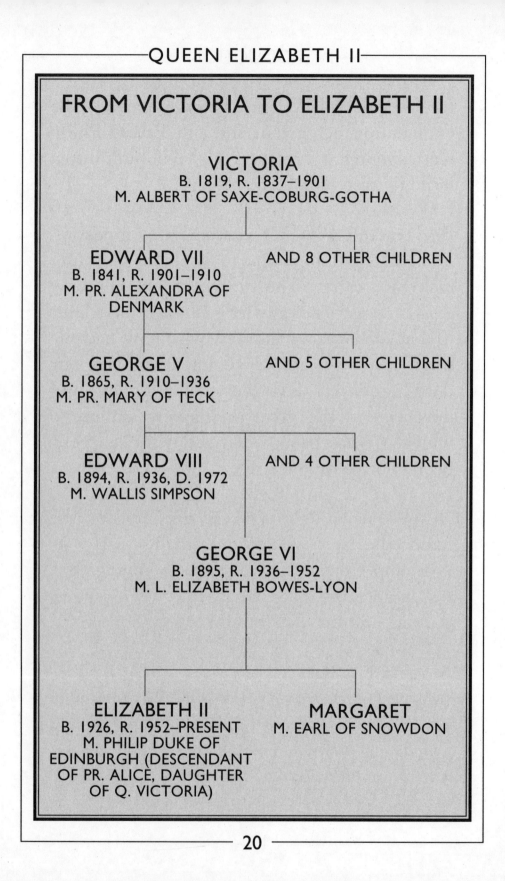

FROM VICTORIA TO ELIZABETH II

VICTORIA
B. 1819, R. 1837–1901
M. ALBERT OF SAXE-COBURG-GOTHA

EDWARD VII
B. 1841, R. 1901–1910
M. PR. ALEXANDRA OF
DENMARK

AND 8 OTHER CHILDREN

GEORGE V
B. 1865, R. 1910–1936
M. PR. MARY OF TECK

AND 5 OTHER CHILDREN

EDWARD VIII
B. 1894, R. 1936, D. 1972
M. WALLIS SIMPSON

AND 4 OTHER CHILDREN

GEORGE VI
B. 1895, R. 1936–1952
M. L. ELIZABETH BOWES-LYON

ELIZABETH II
B. 1926, R. 1952–PRESENT
M. PHILIP DUKE OF
EDINBURGH (DESCENDANT
OF PR. ALICE, DAUGHTER
OF Q. VICTORIA)

MARGARET
M. EARL OF SNOWDON

t was hugely embarrassing that the heavy German aircraft which crossed the Channel in March 1917 to bomb London was called the Gotha G.IV. For wasn't King George V's family part of the House of Saxe-Coburg and Gotha, and wasn't his wife German, too? Yes and yes. And not only was anti-German sentiment at boiling point, but the abdication that very same month of George's cousin, Tsar Nicholas II of Russia, put the frighteners on monarchies all over Europe.

George promptly changed his name to Windsor! Another of his cousins, the emperor Wilhelm

II (nicknamed 'Kaiser Bill', and himself forced to abdicate when Germany lost the war) joked that he was looking forward to seeing a production of Shakespeare's play *The Merry Wives of Saxe-Coburg-Gotha*.

Why Windsor? The medieval castle in Berkshire had a long association with the royal family, and George employed some 660 servants there. Its round tower formed the centrepiece of the badge devised for his new royal House of Windsor.

GEORGE V'S PROCLAMATION

'Now, therefore, We, out of Our Royal Will and Authority, do hereby declare and announce that as from the date of this Our Royal Proclamation Our House and Family shall be styled and known as the House and Family of Windsor, and that all the descendants in the male line of Our said Grandmother Queen Victoria who are subjects of these Realms, other than female descendants who may marry or may have married, shall bear the said Name of Windsor.'

17 July 1917

The novelist H. G. Wells was one of many who had reservations about the royal family, writing about Britain's 'alien and uninspiring court'. The King reacted vigorously (and humorously) to that: 'I may be uninspiring,' he said, 'but I'll be damned if I'm alien!' Hmmm.

STIRRING THE POT

The former British Sea Lord Prince Louis of Battenberg likewise responded to the mood of the times by tranforming himself into a Mountbatten. We've already met his grandson, Philip, who in 1947 married the princess who would become our present Queen. Had it not been for those name changes their wedding, rather than being a Windsor–Mountbatten affair, would have spliced a Saxe-Coburg-Gotha with a Battenberg.

But do you imagine it's that simple? As he was a prince (of Greece and Denmark), Philip had no surname, but he was of the House of Schleswig-Holstein-Sonderburg-Glücksburg, a minor branch of the House of Oldenburg. No wonder he opted for plain Mountbatten! When she came to the throne in 1952, the

Queen (advised by her grandmother Queen Mary and by Prime Minister Winston Churchill) confirmed that her children and their descendants would bear the name of Windsor, to which the forthright Philip is said to have protested: 'I'm nothing but a bloody amoeba . . . the only man in the country not allowed to give his name to his own children.'

In 1960 the Queen relented. In future, she announced, any of her direct descendants not 'enjoying' the title of royal highness, prince or princess would henceforward be known as Mountbatten-Windsor.

ROYAL ROULETTE

Anti-monarchists like to point out the sheer chance by which any particular ruler comes to be on the throne – and that the genetic soup is as likely to produce a bad one as a good one.

Exhibit A is Queen Victoria, who as a young girl can never have expected to rule her country, let alone to remain at the helm for more than 60 years. Her emergence from the dynastic shadows began the hit-and-miss process which 110 years later saw the succession of our present Queen.

Why was Victoria such an unlikely monarch? Because her father, Edward, was the fourth son of George III, and therefore a real outsider in the inheritance stakes. All of his older brothers married, and all of them produced children, but unfortunately not a single one of their offspring was in a position to step up to the plate.

TAIL WAGGING THE DOG

While we're on the subject of breeding, have you ever wondered what the difference is between a German Shepherd dog and an Alsatian?

There isn't one! Just as George V changed his name to avoid any suggestion of being pro-German, so the two World Wars prompted English and American breeders to obscure the fact that the breed was developed by Captain Max von Stephanitz at Karlsruhe in 1899.

Corgis, fortunately, come from Wales . . .

• **George.** The extravagant Prince of Wales, who became George IV in 1820, came closest to providing an heir. He and Queen Caroline notoriously separated very soon after their wedding, but they had a daughter, Charlotte, who would eventually have become queen had she not died from complications after childbirth in 1817.

• **Frederick.** The Duke of York (unhappily pilloried in the nursery rhyme for leading his men to the top of the hill and down again in the Flanders campaign) married a cousin, Princess Frederica Charlotte of Prussia, but the couple soon split up. Frederick had any number of children by other women, but they were of course ruled out from the succession as they were illegitimate. Frederick died while George was still on the throne, and therefore never had a taste of kingship himself.

• **William.** The Duke of Clarence had ten children by Dorothea Bland, better known as the actress Mrs Jordan, but he hadn't married her – and wouldn't have been allowed to in any case. When the death of both Princess Charlotte and his brother Frederick lined him up to become William IV, he cast around desperately for a likely bride. He married Princess Adelaide of Saxe-Meiningen, who at 25 was half his age, but although they lived long and happily together they had only two daughters, both of whom died young.

• **And Edward?** The Duke of Kent had died a few days before his father back in 1820, when his only child Victoria was just eight months old. So it was that when Uncle William died a few weeks after her 18th birthday, the young princess inherited the Crown.

KINGS AND QUEENS OF THE UNITED KINGDOM

• **House of Stuart**
1707*–1714 Anne

• **House of Hanover**
1714–1727 George I
1727–1760 George II
1760–1820 George III
1820–1830 George IV
1830–1837 William IV
1837–1901 Victoria

• **House of Wettin**
(Saxe-Coburg-Gotha)
1901–1910 Edward VII

• **House of Windsor**
1910–1936 George V
1936 Edward VIII
1936–1952 George VI
1952–present Elizabeth II

Queen of England, Scotland and Ireland from 1702.

A QUIVERFUL OF QUEENS

- **Matilda** (ruled 1141). Some say she doesn't count, because she was never crowned, but she was the last heir from the paternal line of William the Conqueror, she ruled for a few months before her cousin Stephen took over, and her eldest son became Henry II.

- **Lady Jane Grey** (1553). Matilda's reign lasted an age compared with hers – just nine days. Poor Jane never wanted to be queen, but it was foisted upon her at the age of 15. Henry VIII's son, Edward VI, had just died, and Protestant sympathisers wanted to stop his older half-sister, the Roman Catholic Mary Tudor, from becoming queen. It didn't work, and in 1554 Jane was beheaded at the Tower of London.

- **Mary I** (1553–1558). A bit of a frightener, especially if you were a Protestant. She earned the nickname 'Bloody Mary' because she was fond of burning her religious enemies at the stake – nearly 300 of them in just a few years. She met her own end, possibly from cancer, during a flu epidemic.

- **Elizabeth I** (1558–1603). The real deal, at last. Henry VIII's daughter by Anne Boleyn was much more restrained than her sister, and her reign is generally remembered for the good things – seafaring dash and daring (epitomised by Sir Francis Drake) and the flourishing of English drama (with Shakespeare leading the way). She never married, and a cult grew up around her of the 'Virgin Queen'.

• **Mary II** (1689–1694). The Protestant Mary and her husband, William of Orange, were co-regents over England, Scotland and Ireland after the so-called Glorious Revolution of 1688 – a bloodless affair which shunted Mary's Catholic father James II & VII out of the country. The pair signed the English Bill of Rights, which promoted a new degree of individual liberty and political democracy.

• **Anne** (Queen of England, Scotland and Ireland 1702–1707; of the United Kingdom, 1707–1714). Mary died, childless, in 1694, and her younger sister followed her to the throne when William III passed on. Since she, too, had no surviving children (though she gave birth 14 times), the Stuart royal line ended with her, and her second cousin George I became the first Hanoverian monarch. Anne posthumously gave her name to a baroque style of architecture.

• **Victoria** (1837–1901). She went one better than Anne and gave her name to an entire age. She oversaw the expansion of the British empire, and in 1876 assumed the title Empress of India. Her reign lasted for all of 63 years and 7 months – a record due to be exceeded by Elizabeth II on the 10th of September 2015.

• **Elizabeth II** (1952–present).

Victoria and her husband, Prince Albert of Saxe-Coburg and Gotha, made sure of providing an heir to the throne by producing no fewer than nine children. They and 26 of the couple's 42 grandchildren married into continental nobility, so earning Victoria the nickname 'the grandmother of Europe'.

There then followed a succession of second children to the throne:

• **Edward VII.** He was a year younger than his sister Victoria, but as a mere woman she had to make way for him. (Never mind: she married Frederick III of Germany, so didn't actually go without.)

• **George V.** His brother Albert, who was 17 months his senior, died of pneumonia a few days after his 28th birthday in 1891.

• **George VI.** As we've seen (page 17), George was propelled into kingship by the abdication of his brother. Yes, Edward VIII *was* king, from 20 January to 11 December 1936, but he was never crowned.

THE WAR AND BEYOND

George VI was a shy man with a debilitating stammer who had never wanted the Crown. That, as the award-winning 2011 film *The King's Speech* demonstrated, made his dutiful decision to accept the burden a form of heroism. The abdication crisis had been a low point for the reputation of the monarchy, not least because Edward and his circle were known to have Nazi sympathies, but when George and Elizabeth opted to stay in London during the dark days of the Blitz rather than retreat to the safety of one of their country estates, the public responded with admiration and affection.

Such was the general atmosphere of goodwill when Elizabeth II came to the throne. Her wedding day had given the people some unwonted glitz and glamour in the dreary aftermath of the war. Now, with the last of the rationing nearly over, her dazzling coronation ceremony surely heralded the dawn of a bright new era.

CORONATION DAY: THE QUEEN LEAVES WESTMINSTER ABBEY IN THE GOLD STATE COACH OF 1762

f 2 June was the greatest day in the 1953 calendar, another event reported that same morning managed the almost impossible – to give the crowning of a new queen a little extra gloss.

On 29 May Edmund Hillary and Tenzing Norgay became the first men known to have reached the summit of the world's highest mountain peak. Hillary was a New Zealander and Tenzing was Nepalese, but what mattered was that this was a British expedition. As a famous *Daily Express* headline had it: 'ALL THIS – AND EVEREST TOO!'

DRAB BRITAIN

The glamour of Coronation Day was all the more dazzling for being set against the colourless background of postwar Britain. Weed-choked bombsites still remained in London and other cities, and the last rationing (on meat and bacon) wouldn't be lifted until 4 July 1954.

Many of the things we take for granted today were luxuries in the early 1950s:

• Only 30 per cent of homes had washing machines, most of them single-tub affairs with a separate hand mangle for wringing out the clothes.

• Only one in ten of us had a telephone, so there were public callboxes everywhere.

• Some 15 per cent had a fridge, making a cool larder essential.

• There were only 1.5 million cars on the roads, compared with 35 million today, but there were plentiful bus and train services.

• A television set (black and white, and only BBC until 1955) was a prized possession – and the Coronation gave a spurt to sales.

The monarchy's fiercest critics concede that the British know how to stage a good pageant, and this was an extravaganza which for sheer over-the-top traditional flummery has never been exceeded in all the intervening years.

The Queen made her way from Buckingham Palace to Westminster Abbey in her golden coach, followed by such a flotilla of similar, if less grand, conveyances that there was a shortage of professional coachmen to man them. (Country squires and millionaire businessmen volunteered to stand in, dressing up as royal servants for the day.)

Three million flag-waving citizens lined the streets, while some 20 million packed into small rooms to watch television sets up and down the land, and another 12 million followed the drama on the 'wireless'.

The Queen's dress, designed by Norman Hartnell, was of white silk, and embroidered with the floral emblems of Commonwealth countries – not only the Tudor rose of England, the Scots thistle, the Welsh leek and the Irish shamrock, but the wattle (Australia), the maple leaf (Canada), the fern (New Zealand), the protea (South Africa), two lotus flowers (India and Ceylon) and wheat, cotton and jute (Pakistan). Hartnell also threw in a four-leaf clover for luck, at a spot where he knew the Queen's hand would come to rest throughout the day.

The ceremony was conducted by the Archbishop of Canterbury, Geoffrey Fisher, before a congregation of 7,500 closely packed guests – 18 inches (45 cm) allowed for each – from all around the world.

SALOTE'S SMILE

One of the most popular foreign dignitaries at the Coronation was Queen Salote of Tonga. A large woman with a huge and winning smile, she rode to the Abbey in a coach whose top she cheerfully refused to close, despite the fact that it was raining.

A quip by the entertainer and humourist Noël Coward would probably have failed to gain currency had it been uttered in our more politically correct times. Asked the identity of a diminutive man sitting next to Salote, he replied on the instant, 'Her lunch'.

A PUSH-START

A hitch at the beginning went unobserved by the watching millions. When the Queen discovered that the friction between her robes and the carpet prevented her moving forward, she whispered urgently to Fisher, 'Get me started!'

A whole succession of robes forced the Queen to be something of a quick-change artiste:

- **Robe of State.** Made of crimson velvet, this was the one that caused the initial bother.

- **Anointing gown.** Simple and plain white.

- **Colobium sindonis (shroud tunic).** A loose undergarment of fine linen, symbolising the derivation of royal authority from the people.

- **Supertunica.** A long coat of gold silk which reached to the ankles.

- **Robe Royal, or Pallium Regale.** The main robe worn during the ceremony and for the actual crowning, this was a four-square mantle lined with crimson silk.

- **Stole Royal or Armilla.** A scarf of gold silk,

embroidered with gold and silver thread and set with jewels, which accompanied the Robe Royal.

- **Purple surcoat.**

- **Imperial Robe.** The last of all, worn on the way out of the Abbey.

And here's a checklist of the Queen's Coronation regalia:
- **The Orb**
- **St Edward's Crown**
- **Imperial Crown of State**
- **The Sword of State**
- **The Sword of Mercy**
- **The Sword of Spiritual Justice**
- **The Sword of Temporal Justice**
- **The Jewelled Sword**
- **The Ampulla**
- **The Spurs**
- **The Royal Sceptre**
- **St Edward's Staff**
- **The Sceptre with the Dove.**

A special set of four postage stamps was issued in the UK, each designed by a different artist. Edmund Dulac, who created the 1s 3d (6.25p) stamp, had also devised the 1937 stamp for the coronation of the Queen's parents. Unhappily he died, at the age of 71, just a few days before the 1953 set was issued.

The Coronation was a great excuse for a bit of fun, at home and abroad. Street parties were organised throughout the nation, while in London there was an RAF fly-past along the Mall and thousands enjoyed a firework display on the Victoria Embankment. Canadian soldiers serving in the Korean War played their part by firing red, white and blue smoke shells at the enemy – and, of course, knocking back celebratory rum rations.

UNEASY LIES THE HEAD...

There were several rehearsals of the coronation ceremony, sometimes with the Duchess of Norfolk standing in for the Queen, but Elizabeth herself prepared for the difficult task of walking with the heavy (2 lb, 0.91 kg) Imperial State Crown on her head by wearing it as she went about her day-to-day business at Buckingham Palace.

Odd as it seems, she could sometimes be seen sporting the grand 'titfer' (2,868 diamonds, 273 pearls, 17 sapphires, 11 emeralds, 5 rubies) while working at her desk or reading a newspaper at the breakfast table.

THE WORLD IN 1953

January
- USA develops a hydrogen bomb.
- Mau Mau uprising in Kenya.
- Premieres of Samuel Beckett's *Waiting for Godot* and Arthur Miller's *The Crucible*.
- Floods kill hundreds on the east coast of Britain.

February
- James Watson and Francis Crick announce their discovery of the structure of DNA.

March
- Death of Soviet dictator Joseph Stalin; Nikita Khrushchev becomes First Secretary of the Soviet Communist Party.

April
- Ian Fleming publishes the first James Bond novel, *Casino Royale*.

May
- British expedition scales Everest.

June
- Elizabeth II's coronation.
- Communists Julius and Ethel Rosenberg executed in USA for spying.

July
- European Economic Community (EEC) holds its first meeting in Strasbourg.
- Korean War ends.

August
- Soviet Union develops a hydrogen bomb.

September
- End of sugar rationing in the UK.

October
- First use of random-access memory (RAM) in a commercial computer.

November
- Piltdown Man (a supposed early hominid excavated in Sussex in 1912) finally exposed as a hoax.
- England's footballers lose 6–3 to Hungary at Wembley, their first home defeat by a European team.

December
- Hugh Hefner publishes the first issue of *Playboy* magazine.

AMONG MY SOUVENIRS

It was a good opportunity, too, for businessmen with an eye to the main chance. All sorts of souvenirs were created, from the relatively expensive (plates, bowls, silver spoons) through the workaday (mugs, biscuit and toffee tins, trays, tea strainers, pocket knives) and the sartorial (ties, scarves, handkerchiefs) to the bizarre (a plastic paintbox in the shape of a crown, a doll's dressing-table brush set).

FIT FOR A QUEEN?

But perhaps the most lasting tribute to the great day is a dish which has become a fixture on the British menu – and which diners tend either to love or to loathe. Designed especially for 350 guests at the Coronation luncheon, it was officially named *Poulet Reine Elizabeth* (the French soubriquet gave it a bit of swank in those culinarily deprived times), but has ever since been known as Coronation chicken.

This lightly curried concoction was the creation of Rosemary Hume, who ran the London Cordon Bleu Cookery School with the royal florist-cum-foodie Constance Spry, author of the wartime book *Come into the Garden, Cook*, which had encouraged British housewives to grow and prepare their own food.

According to Hume's niece, her inspiration had come from a favourite dish of Queen Adelaide, wife of William IV – chicken with a curry and apricot butter, as devised by the 19th-century celebrity cookery writer Mrs (Harriet) De Salis. The fact that it was served cold was no doubt an added attraction: the guests ate in the Great Hall of Westminster School, where the kitchen facilities were minimal.

The authentic recipe can be found in *The Constance Spry Cookery Book* by Constance Spry and Rosemary Hume (Grub Street, 2014).

WHAT THEY PLAYED THEN

Ten hit songs in Coronation year

- *I Believe* (Frankie Laine)

- *Because You're Mine* (Mario Lanza)

- *The Song from Moulin Rouge* (Mantovani and his Orchestra)

- *You Belong to Me* (Jo Stafford)

- *Here in My Heart* (Al Martino)

- *Pretend* (Nat King Cole)

- *She Wears Red Feathers* (Guy Mitchell)

- *Outside of Heaven* (Eddie Fisher)

- *How Much is that Doggie in the Window?* (Lita Roza)

- *O Mein Papa* (Eddie Calvert)

THE CORONATION OATH

Responding to questions by the Archbishop, the Queen promised to 'cause law and justice, in mercy, to be executed' in all her judgements, to 'maintain the laws of God and the true profession of the Gospel' and to 'maintain and preserve inviolably the settlement of the Church of England, and the doctrine, worship, discipline and government thereof, as by law established in England'.

She also solemnly promised and swore 'to govern the peoples of the United Kingdom of Great Britain and Northern Ireland, Canada, Australia, New Zealand, the Union of South Africa, Pakistan and Ceylon', together with all her other 'possessions and the other territories to any of them belonging or pertaining, according to their respective laws and customs'.

On that rapidly changing wider world she was soon to attempt the sprinkling of her royal stardust.

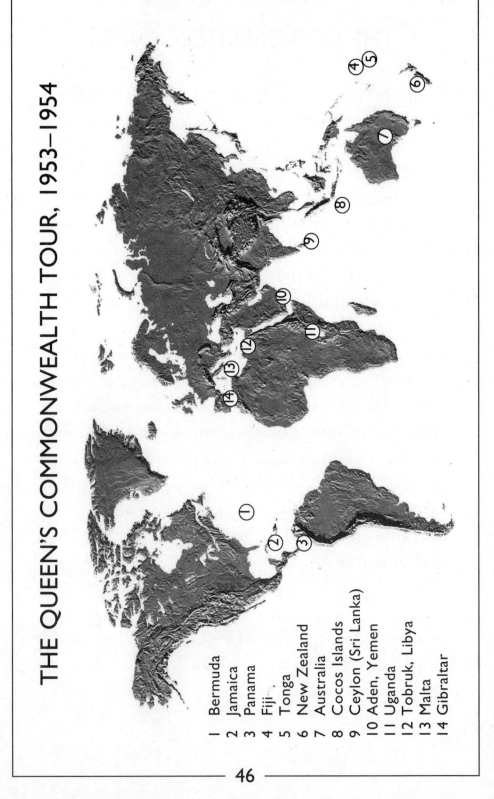

THE QUEEN'S COMMONWEALTH TOUR, 1953–1954

1 Bermuda
2 Jamaica
3 Panama
4 Fiji
5 Tonga
6 New Zealand
7 Australia
8 Cocos Islands
9 Ceylon (Sri Lanka)
10 Aden, Yemen
11 Uganda
12 Tobruk, Libya
13 Malta
14 Gibraltar

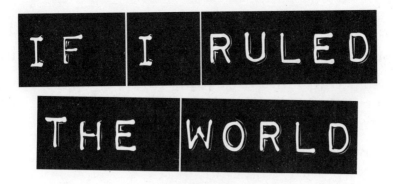

The first Queen Elizabeth established her authority by making an annual 'progress' to the towns and stately homes of southern England. Her namesake has regularly shown the flag to a much larger and more scattered community all over the globe. Only months after her coronation, she began a six-month tour of the Commonwealth which encompassed 14 countries in the West Indies, Australasia, Asia and Africa. By the time of her Diamond Jubilee in 2012 she had made more than 250 visits overseas, and was comfortably the most travelled head of state in history.

For that first jaunt in November 1953 the royal party set out on the liner SS *Gothic*, with a full complement of followers:

- two ladies-in-waiting
- three private secretaries
- the Master of the Household
- two equerries
- 20 officials and staff
- a press secretary
- 72 naval staff
- and the band of the Royal Marines.

FAR AND WIDE

The Queen's 1953–1954 Commonwealth tour encompassed 43,000 miles (69,000 km) in six months:

- **Bermuda:** 24–25 November
- **Jamaica:** 25–27 November
- **Fiji:** 17–19 December
- **Tonga:** 19–20 December
- **New Zealand:** 23 December – 30 January
- **Australia:** 3 February – 1 April
- **Cocos Islands:** 5 April
- **Ceylon** (now Sri Lanka): 10–21 April
- **Aden:** 27 April
- **Uganda:** 28–30 April
- **Malta:** 3–7 May
- **Gibraltar:** 10 May.

The baggage was estimated to weigh 12 tonnes, the wardrobe alone consisting of more than a hundred dresses – including the Coronation dress, which the Queen wore on three separate occasions.

Apart from sailing some 30,000 miles (48,300 km), she travelled an estimated 10,000 miles (16,100 km) by plane, 2,500 (4,000) by rail and 900 (1,450) by car.

Once the *Gothic* had reached Australia it was loaded up with pre-packaged food, partly because there was a polio scare in the western states. (Royal hand-shaking was therefore out of bounds.) The stores included:

- 10,000 cartons of canned fruit
- 5,000 cartons of tomato juice
- 1,500 cases of canned meat
- 3,237 bags of milk powder.

Still, the Queen has had to eat some strange meals in her time. As protocol rules that the cameras never watch her eating in public, we can only imagine the expression on her face while tucking into the likes of barbecued turtle, coral worms, rat or roast bat.

NOT SO GREAT BRITAIN

Had she come to the throne a few years earlier, Elizabeth would have inherited Victoria's grand title 'Empress of India'. But the world had moved on and the grandeur was fast departing. India had won independence in 1947 (Philip's uncle, Viscount Louis Mountbatten, was the last British governor-general there), and within a few more years Prime Minister Harold Macmillan would be making his famous speech about the 'wind of change' blowing through Africa. With 'empire' a dirty word, Britain's power in the world was in obvious decline.

The end of British influence, then? By no means! In 1949 her father had become the first Head of the Commonwealth, and now Elizabeth found herself with the same title, and the constitutional monarch not only of the United Kingdom, but of Australia, Canada, New Zealand, South Africa, Pakistan and Ceylon, too. As other former colonies gained their independence over the years, she would become queen of 25 more.

The Commonwealth was designed as a gathering of equals, but the razzmatazz surrounding royal visits to around 130 countries during her reign suggests that one of them remains perhaps more equal than others.

AN ASSASSINATION ATTEMPT?

Was there an attempt on the Queen's life during her 1970 trip to Australia?

Years later, a former senior New South Wales detective told the **Lithgow Mercury** that a large log had been placed on the railway tracks just before the royal train arrived. It became lodged under the train, which skidded for 200 yards (180 metres) before coming to a stop. Had the train not been travelling more slowly than usual, it would have plunged off the tracks and into an embankment.

The **Mercury**'s managing editor admitted that the paper had kept the incident quiet at the time in order to save Australia embarrassment.

THE COMMONWEALTH

Few areas of the world atlas are now coloured pink to signify British ownership, but here's a staggering figure: some 30 per cent of the world's population live in the Commonwealth of Nations – a total of more than two billion people.

This unique 'free association of independent nations' emerged from the crumbling of the British Empire, but it's not a political union and it has a completely different ethos. Although English is its common language, the Queen is its symbolic head by agreement rather than by right, and its working chief is the Secretary-General.

While 16 'Commonwealth realms' recognise the Queen as their head of state, five countries have their own monarchs and another 33 are republics.

At the time of the Diamond Jubilee there were 54 member states, and all but two (Mozambique and Rwanda) were formerly part of the British Empire.

Some member countries, such as Canada and Australia, cover a huge area, while others – with an equal voice in the debating chamber – are tiny: Nauru in the Pacific is the world's smallest island nation, measuring just 8 square miles (21 sq km).
The Singapore Declaration of 1971 (refined by the Harare Declaration 20 years later) established the goals and values of the Commonwealth, including

the promotion of democracy, human rights, good governance, the rule of law, individual liberty, egalitarianism, free trade, multilateralism and world peace.

Commonwealth countries are not considered 'foreign' to one another, and their mutual diplomatic missions are therefore designated as high commissions rather than embassies.

Of course there are sometimes fallings-out, as in all close families – a notable example being South Africa's expulsion in 1961 because of its racist apartheid policy. It returned to the fold in 1994.

Nigeria, Pakistan (twice), Fiji (twice) and Zimbabwe have at various times been suspended for violating the principles of democracy, and in 2003 Zimbabwe withdrew from the Commonwealth altogether.

The best known of the organisation's many activities are the Commonwealth Games, staged at different venues every four years.

'The Commonwealth makes the world safe for diversity.'

Nelson Mandela

'HOW VERY KIND OF YOU!'

The royal entourage travels loaded with gifts (for the visit to China in 1986 there were no fewer than 12 boxes of them, packed in glass-fibre cases) and the Queen receives a huge array of them in return. Here are a few of the living presents on which her majesty has smiled her gratitude, some of which were given a home in London Zoo:

• tortoises (the Seychelles)
• a bull elephant (Cameroon)
• jaguars and sloths (Brazil)
• black beavers (Canada).

Some gifts have been awkwardly perishable, such as eggs, pineapples, trout and prawns. Others must have looked rather out of place in Windsor Castle or Buckingham Palace. Here's a cabinet of curiosities:

• lacrosse sticks
• a box of snail shells
• Zulu chess sets
• Maori feather cloaks and boomerangs
• cowboy boots
• totem poles
• a whale's tooth.

DID HE REALLY SAY THAT?

Having her husband alongside her in support is, no doubt, a blessing to the Queen on her arduous royal journeys, but it has sometimes proved to be a mixed one. Prince Philip is well known for his colourful off-the-cuff remarks – so much so that one website actually provides a useful map of the world showing which of their host nations he has risked offending over the years.

Mind you, his defenders will say that a little humorous straight-talking doesn't go amiss.

On a visit to Slovenia in 2008, for instance, he told a university professor hoping to attract more people to visit her country that 'Tourism is just national prostitution. We don't need any more tourists. They ruin cities.' (For the record, she later said the prince was charming, very funny and had a twinkle in his eye.)

As we're spoilt for choice, we'll give you our top ten one-liners from a man who acknowledges that people think of him as 'a cantankerous old sod'.

TEN OF THE BEST PHILIPISMS

1. *Canada:* 'We don't come here for our health. We can think of other ways of enjoying ourselves.'

2. *To the president of **Nigeria**, dressed in formal white robes:* 'You look like you're ready for bed.'

3. *To British students in **China**:* 'If you stay here much longer you'll go home slitty-eyed.'

4. *Examining an old-fashioned fuse box in a factory near Edinburgh:* 'It looks as if it was put in by an Indian.'

5. *To an aboriginal leader in **Australia**:* 'Do you still throw spears at each other?'

6. *To a student who had been trekking in **Papua New Guinea**:* 'You managed not to get eaten, then?'

7. *After accepting a conservation award in **Thailand**:* 'Your country is one of the most notorious centres of trading in endangered species in the world.'

8. *To a native of the **Cayman Islands**:* 'Aren't you descended from pirates?'

9. *To an Englishman in **Hungary**:* 'You can't have been here that long – you haven't got a pot belly.'

10. *To a driving instructor in **Scotland**:* 'How do you keep your natives off the booze long enough to get them through the test?'

DUTIFUL DUKE

Prince Philip, Duke of Edinburgh (to give him his usual title) holds the ranks of Admiral of the Fleet, Field Marshal and Marshal of the Royal Air Force, and Captain-General of the Royal Marines.

He is president or patron of some 800 organisations, with an emphasis on industry, sport, education and the environment: he was the President of the Worldwide Fund for Nature from 1981 to 1996.

In 1956 he founded the Duke of Edinburgh's Award to promote among young people 'a sense of responsibility to themselves and their communities'.

AN ISLAND GOD

And yet, amazingly, on the Pacific island of Tanna in Vanuatu, Prince Philip is regarded as nothing less than a god.

For centuries the people had believed an ancient story about a pale-skinned son of a mountain spirit who would sail the seas to find a powerful woman to marry. During the 1960s the legend became associated with the Prince – who had, of course, found just such a wife.

After their ancestral spirit paid an official visit to the island alongside the Queen in 1974 they sent him a traditional pig-killing club, and their proudest possession is a photograph which shows him holding it. They celebrate his birthday with a feast which includes the ceremonial drinking of *kava*, an intoxicating brew made from the roots of a pepper tree.

Anthropologists describe the so-called Prince Philip Movement as a cargo cult which preserves the indigenous culture by filtering into it aspects of the modern world. What the Prince makes of it, nobody knows.

THE FIRST ROYAL WALKABOUT

Since royal tours were more starchy affairs in the early days of Elizabeth's reign, her decision to mingle with the crowds, rather than simply shake hands with the bigwigs, was a much- heralded feature of her visit to Australia and New Zealand in 1970.

Young Australian aborigines traditionally took to the wilderness to follow the paths of their ancestors as a rite of passage, a practice known as 'going walkabout'. The media immediately borrowed the term for the first of the Queen's meet-the-people forays – and so they've been known ever since.

CHILLED BY KINDNESS

Making sure that the Queen is comfortable on her overseas tours requires a veritable army of underlings performing their tasks without a hitch. She has to have at least three outfits available each day (plus mourning clothes in case of a disaster), and her 'travelling yeoman' is charged with making sure that the royal luggage arrives in the Queen's apartment before she does.

Too much TLC can cause problems, however. Anxious hosts in Nigeria once turned up the air-conditioning in her rooms so extravagantly that her clothes froze on their hangers.

WE ARE SAILING

As far as we know Prince Philip has made no derogatory remarks about Clydeside shipbuilders, which is just as well – after all, they provided the royal couple with a splendidly luxurious billet for their many world travels.

The Royal Yacht *Britannia* was launched at John Brown's shipyard in 1953, and was ready to bring the Queen and her entourage home from that first Commonwealth trip the following spring. It would serve them for all of 44 years, travel more than a million miles (1.6 million km) and call in at 600 ports in 135 countries.

BRITANNIA FACTS AND FIGURES

- The royal yacht was a venue for official entertaining as well as being a royal home-from-home. The state apartments catered for up to 250 guests.

- The wheel in the wheelhouse came from George V's racing yacht *Britannia;* the binnacle (compass housing) on the veranda deck was originally in George IV's *Royal George* (built in 1817); and the furniture in the state apartments included a small gimbal table designed by Queen Victoria's husand, Prince Albert.

- Her captain had the rank of Commodore, and all the crew (19 officers and 217 Royal Yachtsmen) were volunteers, who joined from the General Service of the Royal Navy.

- Royal Yachtsmen had a distinctive uniform, finished off at the back with a black silk bow of the kind originally worn in mourning for Prince Albert.

- No shouted orders were given on board, so as not to disturb the royals. Hand signals were used instead.

A RAPTUROUS WELCOME

The Queen returned from her Commonwealth tour in May 1954 to scenes scarcely imaginable today. Ships' sirens and factory hooters blasted a welcome, and thousands of people lined the banks of the Thames to watch *Britannia* sail in. A huge red-and-white banner was attached to Tower Bridge, bearing the words 'Welcome Home'.

Once having disembarked at Westminster, the royal party drove to Buckingham Palace in three carriages, while thousands of cheering flag-wavers (some had been up all night to make sure of a good vantage point) lined the clamorous streets. No sooner had the doors of the Palace closed than a great cry went up: 'We want the Queen!'

One glimpse wasn't enough. Elizabeth, Philip and their two children, Charles and Anne, were persuaded to make no fewer than four appearances on the Palace balcony, the last shortly before midnight, and the crowds at last began to disperse only after the floodlights had been turned off.

So, in effect, began the domestic reign of Elizabeth II. Her people, freshly delivered from the toils of war, seemed in a mood to celebrate the homecoming of their young, newly crowned Queen and her handsome consort as symbols of a comforting renewal.

Habitual deference to authority, though on the wane, could still be relied on to enthuse large swathes of the populace for a special occasion. The testing times were yet to come...

THE QUEEN AND THE DUKE OF EDINBURGH LEAVING CHURCH

F ew people brought up in the early years of the Queen's reign could ever have imagined her dropping into a Glasgow council flat to have a natter with its occupants over a cup of tea. True, her parents had mingled with the East End crowds after the bombing raids of the war, but that was a rare expression of solidarity in a crisis – royalty was otherwise accustomed to maintaining its regal distance.

That was all to change. Carefully stage-managed 'getting to know you' events would eventually become commonplace.

THE QUEEN'S ROLE

As a constitutional monarch, Elizabeth II has a largely symbolic function. Her executive powers as head of state are restricted by the laws of the land – the royal website describes her other, 'head of the nation' role as providing 'a focus of national identity and unity'.

On paper she has more power than she actually dare use. She could, for instance, refuse a government's request to dissolve Parliament and call an election. She also has the right to choose the prime minister, a potentially delicate matter whenever there is a hung parliament. In reality she carefully consults and advises, without interfering in the democratic process.

The Queen also has residual powers, known as 'the royal prerogative', to enact legislation, award honours, sign treaties and declare war. This prerogative is sometimes used not by herself but by politicians eager to take action without first having their policy approved by Parliament – as when Edward Heath took Britain into the Common Market in 1972, and when Margaret Thatcher went to war in the Falklands ten years later.

Representing Britain to the rest of the world, the Queen receives foreign ambassadors and high commissioners and entertains visiting heads of state. She is also the monarch of 16 former British colonies, and (as we've seen) head of the Commonwealth.

For monarchists determined to preserve the institution in an increasingly unceremonial age this intimate glad-handing of the public threatened to be a two-edged sword: as it hacked away outdated layers of protocol separating the Queen from her subjects, wouldn't it also sever the precious thread of deference to the Crown?

I HAVE A DREAM

Deference or not, it's a strange fact that a great many people report dreaming about the Queen. Here's a small sample drawn from the Web:

- One person dreamed of meeting the Queen several times, in a friend's kitchen. At first the Queen was friendly, but in the last meeting the dreamer became exasperated with her and lost her temper.

- In another dream, the Queen was distressed, complaining that she had no friends and that Tony Blair (British Prime Minister 1997–2007) had deceived her.

- Someone else dreamed that the Queen was sitting beside him as he drove a train through the Highlands of Scotland. The dream stayed with him for a long time afterwards.

- One person dreamed of being invited to stay at Buckingham Palace, and worrying about how to behave, what to wear and who to talk to.

WALKING BACKWARDS

Laughable as it may seem, it was until recently a subject's duty to walk backwards when leaving the Queen's presence, a medieval custom reintroduced by Edward VII at the beginning of the 20th century.

The practice was discontinued in August 2009, ostensibly to comply with health and safety regulations. For traditional diehards, however, the good news is that three individuals will still have to keep in training: the marshal of the diplomatic corps, the Queen's equerry and the lord chancellor, who has to manage the feat while descending the steps from the throne at the State Opening of Parliament.

MANY A SLIP

Most of us will never bump into her, but as the odds of entertaining the monarch have narrowed somewhat over the years you're advised to mug up on our Very Peculiar History guide to royal etiquette just in case:

- Everyone (even Prince Philip, it seems) has to stand up when the Queen enters a room. We're told that's because she's never off duty.

- Men should either bow from the shoulders or 'bob' from the neck. Women should curtsey – but, again, a little bob will do.

- The upper-class response to 'How d'you do?' is a repetition of the phrase, rather than 'Pleased to meet you.'

- Address the Queen first as 'Your Majesty', and thereafter as 'Ma'am', making sure to rhyme it with 'jam', not 'smarm'.

- If she offers her hand you should, of course, accept – but by touching it briefly rather than giving it a hearty shake.

- Everyone has to stop eating when the Queen has finished her last mouthful.

- More bows and curtseys, please, when she leaves. Oh, and revert to saying 'Your Majesty' when it's time to say goodbye.

The comforting advice from a Buckingham Palace spokesman is 'just be yourself' – although that might prove a little difficult under the circumstances.

THE ROYAL MAUNDY SERVICE

One of the Queen's annual duties is to distribute so-called 'Maundy money' on the day before Good Friday. These four small silver coins (legal tender, but not circulated because of their value) are symbolic alms granted to elderly people, who also receive small sums of money in lieu of the clothing and food that the sovereign handed out in days gone by.

The Royal Maundy service is held in a different cathedral every year, and the recipients of the coins (a penny, tuppence, threepence and fourpence) are chosen for the service given to their churches in the diocese.

IN ONE'S GARDEN

It was Queen Victoria who first held garden parties for selected members of the public at Buckingham Palace, and the Queen now stages three each year, plus another at Holyroodhouse in Scotland.

The recipient of the invitation is expected to reply by presenting his or her compliments to the Lord Chamberlain, expressing 'the honour to obey Her Majesty's command'.

These are opportunities for worthies from all walks of life, and from communities all round Britain (some 8,000 at a time), to dress in their summer finery – men in morning dress, lounge suits or uniform, women in afternoon dress, usually with hats and gloves – and to munch sandwiches and cakes on the lawn.

The Queen and Prince Philip circulate among the guests, with random presentations giving everyone a small chance of catching the royal ear. Bands play throughout the event, a final playing of the national anthem signalling that the two-hour fest is over.

This genteel British event is meticulously organised (don't be surprised to see police marksmen up on the roof), but it's had its hiccups over the years:

• In 2003 17-year-old Barney Keen, who had come with his parents, dropped his trousers for a bet and ran across the lawn, slapping his bare bottom and shouting 'Wahey!' He was wrestled to the ground by a yeoman of the guard. The Queen was reported to be 'amused', but his parents certainly weren't.

• In 2005 it was claimed that the parties were costing the royal family half a million pounds a year above budget. Greedy guests were each consuming, on average, 14 portions of sandwiches, scones, cakes and ice cream.

• The leader of the British National Party was banned from attending in 2010 after describing his invitation as a 'highly symbolic breakthrough' and asking supporters to email questions for him to put to the Queen. He had been invited as an MEP for North West England, but the Palace felt he had 'overtly' used the invitation for political purposes.

DOWNING STREET DOZEN

By the time of her Diamond Jubilee the Queen had appointed 12 UK prime ministers, only two fewer than the record holder, George III:

Winston Churchill	1952–1955
Anthony Eden	1955–1957
Harold Macmillan	1957–1963
Alec Douglas-Home	1963–1964
Harold Wilson	1964–1970
	and 1974–1976
Edward Heath	1970–1974
James Callaghan	1976–1979
Margaret Thatcher	1979–1990
John Major	1990–1997
Tony Blair	1997–2007
Gordon Brown	2007–2010
David Cameron	2010–present

A GUARDSMAN'S 'BULL'

One royal guardsman fondly remembers the Queen's visit to inspect the stable yard at Whitehall.

Though rehearsals had been carried out for several weeks before the event, with much marching and drilling and shouting of orders, it was not until the actual day that the guardsmen were informed of the identity of their distinguished visitor.

By the time the Queen arrived, the stable yard had been scrubbed so thoroughly that it was difficult to imagine it in its usual filthy state. A well-behaved horse was brought out, and a smartly turned-out detachment of soldiers approached the Queen with an impeccably clean carrot on a silver dish.

The carrot was presented to Her Majesty with all due ceremony. Then the Queen – who is, of course, thoroughly familiar with horses – popped it into the horse's mouth.

Few people appreciate the weeks of planning that go into a simple event of this kind.

SPICK AND SPAN

The Queen and other members of the royal family pay a staggering 3,000 visits a year the length and breadth of the United Kingdom – and she herself accounts for more than 400 of that total.

What impression she gets of day-to-day life in her kingdom is perhaps difficult to gauge. As in many a historical costume drama, everything she sees is incredibly clean and tidy, with splashings of fresh paint and a good deal of spit-and-polish – although tales of coal being painted white to spare royal frowns are, disappointingly, nothing but urban myths.

It's not even true that the Queen takes her own lavatory seat with her. ('Only Prince Charles does that,' said a Palace spokesman.)

While schools, hospitals, military units and community schemes are regular features of her busy agenda, the Queen's itineraries have also included the sets of television soap operas, a Welsh power station, a mosque, Hindu and Sikh temples and a London bus depot – not to speak of that Glasgow council flat, where Mrs Susan McCarron later told the media that she hadn't been at all nervous about having the monarch to tea: 'She was asking about the house and how long I had lived here, where I lived before. I found her very easy to talk to.'

It was during the 1960s that the royal family had first begun to loosen up, recognising that the world about it was changing fast and that the very existence of the monarchy depended on its moving with the times.

THE ROYAL TRAIN

Although the Queen uses RAF planes and helicopters for many of her visits, she frequently boards the royal train for her cross-country journeys. Locomotives painted in the royal household's claret livery pull up to nine carriages, including luxury lounges, bedrooms, kitchens and dining cars, as well as offices and sleeping quarters for staff.

Any young lad (or lass) who still has the dream of becoming a train driver should know that standards are incredibly high on the royal engine. The necessary skills include 'the ability to make a station stop within six inches [15 cm] of the designated position'.

SWINGING BRITAIN

The sixties were the decade in which the young began to find their own voice – and an increasing amount of spending money. No longer simply junior clones of their parents, they found their own music (the Beatles and the Rolling Stones), displayed their own fashions (Carnaby Street was *the* place to shop) and generally cocked a snook at authority (an attitude exemplified in the new satirical magazine *Private Eye* and its TV counterpart *That Was The Week That Was*).

It was a time of protests (against nuclear weapons and the Vietnam war), of scandal (the Christine Keeler affair) and of seismic social change (the introduction of the pill and the legalisation of both abortion and homosexuality). Add to this the determination of Harold Wilson's Labour government to put scientific progress at the forefront of its policies, and it was little wonder that the monarchy began to seem decidedly creaky, old-fashioned and even unnecessary.

ELIZABETH II FACT FILE

- The Queen's official title is Queen of the United Kingdom of Great Britain and Northern Ireland.

- She was born at 17 Bruton Street, Mayfair (the London home of her maternal grandparents), at 2.40 a.m. on 21 April 1926.

- As a girl during the Second World War she acted in several pantomimes at Windsor Castle, once playing the part of Prince Florizel in *Cinderella*.

- She first travelled on the London Underground in May 1939, with her governess Crawfie and Princess Margaret.

- She doesn't need a passport when travelling abroad.

- She's a keen photographer, who enjoys taking pictures of her family.

- The first football match she attended was the 1953 'Matthews final' at Wembley, in which Blackpool beat Bolton Wanderers 4–3.

- She speaks fluent French and doesn't need an interpreter.

- She can't be prosecuted for not wearing a seat belt when out for a drive.

- Cars that she uses on official business do not carry number plates.

- She never wears a hat after 6.00 pm.

- She officially owns all mute swans 'living in open water', as well as all the sturgeons, whales and dolphins in the waters around the UK.

- She has sent some 110,000 congratulatory telegrams to UK and Commonwealth centenarians, and more than 520,000 to couples celebrating their diamond wedding anniversary.

- Because of her ATS training (see page 15), she knows how to change a car wheel.

1960S BRITAIN

1960 Harold Macmillan's 'Wind of Change' speech; *Lady Chatterley* trial.

1961 The Beatles appear at the Cavern, Liverpool; contraceptive pill goes on sale; 1,300 CND protesters arrested in Trafalgar Square; first issue of *Private Eye* magazine.

1962 Satirical TV programme *That Was The Week That Was* launched.

1963 Spy Kim Philby defects to the USSR; Dr Beeching axes many railway lines; defence minister John Profumo resigns over Christine Keeler affair.

1964 *Top of the Pops* first broadcast; Mods and Rockers clash in Brighton.

1965 Death penalty abolished for murder; Mary Quant introduces the miniskirt; funeral of Sir Winston Churchill.

1966 England win World Cup; 116 schoolchildren die in Aberfan disaster.

1967 Abortion and homosexuality legalised in England and Wales.

1968 Hundreds arrested during anti-Vietnam War protest at US Embassy.

1969 Concorde's first supersonic flight.

POMP AND CIRCUMSTANCE

One royal response to all this innovation was decidedly retro: to reassert the glory of the institution by staging another of those grand ceremonies to which the British people are so susceptible.

The vehicle for this lavish display was the investiture of the heir to the throne as Prince of Wales in July 1969. Princess Margaret's celebrity photographer husband, Lord Snowdon, played a part in arranging the event, and he attempted to modernise it to some extent, designing a simple slate dais with a perspex canopy for the ceremony.

He would, nevertheless, later describe the traditional trappings as 'bogus as hell'. He had designed his own uniform to play the role of Constable of Caernarfon Castle, and it made him look like 'a cinema usherette from the 1950s or the panto character Buttons'.

Prince Charles had mugged up on his Welsh in the weeks before the ceremony, so that he could respond in both languages, but the investiture was unpopular with Welsh nationalists, and on the eve of the ceremony two men were killed while planting a bomb.

'By far the most moving and meaningful moment,' the 20-year-old prince wrote in his diary, 'came when I put my hand between Mummy's and swore to be her liege man of life and limb.'

THE ABERFAN DISASTER

On Friday 21 October 1966, after a period of heavy rain, a colliery spoil-heap collapsed above the Welsh village of Aberfan. Some 40,000 cubic metres of mining-waste slurry slid down the hill and engulfed a farm, a row of houses and Pantglas Junior School. Of the 144 people killed, 116 were schoolchildren.

Prince Philip and Lord Snowdon quickly joined rescue workers at the scene, but it was a week before the Queen herself arrived. She was criticised for being out of touch with the people — and was later said to have regarded the delay as the greatest mistake of her reign.

Like the ceremony itself, this 'mummy and liege' language may evoke another age, but the occasion was relayed on television to 19 million people in Britain and 500 million around the world. The panoply of royalty had triumphed again.

JUST LIKE US?

A very different royal response to the changing times, and one promoted by the Palace's new press secretary William Heseltine, was the ground-breaking (some would say disastrous) decision to invite the television cameras to follow the Queen and her family both at work and at play.

The film *Royal Family*, shown shortly before the 1969 investiture, was a 105-minute fly-on-the-wall documentary with an appealing underlying message: richer and grander these people may be, but at heart they're really just like the rest of us.

One of her biographers has claimed that the Queen regretted her decision, but too late – the genie was now out of the bottle.

Among the 'intimate' family scenes:

- The Queen pays a visit to her dogs at Sandringham.

- The family enjoys a barbecue lunch in the grounds at Balmoral, with Prince Philip and Princess Anne as cooks.

- Prince Charles is playing the cello when a string snaps and pings a furious little Prince Edward in the face.

- Prince Andrew kicks a football.

- At breakfast, the Queen tells an anecdote about a dignitary falling over in front of Queen Victoria.

- The Queen rummages in her purse to buy sweets for Edward in a Balmoral sweet shop.

Philip's use of the F-word about the Queen's corgis was, of course, edited out, but the occasional frank comment surprisingly survived uncut.

Philip on George VI: 'He had very odd habits. Sometimes I thought he was mad.'

The Queen: 'How do you keep a straight face when a footman tells you: "Your Majesty, your next audience is with a gorilla"? It was an official visitor, but he looked just like a gorilla.'

The celebrated wildlife broadcaster David Attenborough, then controller of the BBC 2 television channel, accused the film's producer, Richard Cawson, of 'killing' the monarchy.

'The whole institution depends on mystique and the tribal chief in his hut,' he wrote. 'If any member of the tribe ever sees inside the hut, then the whole system of the tribal chiefdom is damaged and the tribe eventually disintegrates.'

The Queen and her advisers clearly agreed with him, because 'Corgi and Beth' (as satirists unkindly dubbed the documentary) was very soon removed from circulation. As late as 2011, only a 90-second clip of it was allowed to be shown during a royal exhibition at the National Portait Gallery.
Twenty-five years on

1970S BRITAIN

1970 Voting age reduced from 21 to 18; Rhodesia (now Zimbabwe) breaks ties with the Crown.

1971 Decimal currency introduced; Divorce Reform Act allows fault-free divorce; Open University admits first students.

1972 'Bloody Sunday' in Northern Ireland.

1973 Value-Added Tax (VAT) introduced; British Library established.

1974 Three-day week introduced during coal miners' strike; IRA bombs in London.

1975 Sex Discrimination Act and Equal Pay Act come into force; first Yorkshire Ripper murder.

1976 Cod War between Britain and Iceland; heatwave brings worst drought since 1720s.

1977 Firemen go on strike; undertakers' strike leaves 800 bodies unburied.

1978 *The Times* newspaper closed by industrial dispute; Louise Brown is first human born from in vitro fertilisation.

1979 Widespread strikes in 'Winter of Discontent'; Margaret Thatcher becomes Britain's first woman prime minister; Lord Mountbatten is assassinated by the IRA.

CRY TREASON!

In May 1968, at a time of economic crisis, the head of the IPC magazine empire, Cecil King, called for a meeting with Earl Mountbatten of Burma, Prince Philip's uncle.

To Mountbatten's amazement, King explained that he was expecting the government to collapse and for there to be bloodshed on the streets. In that event, would Mountbatten agree to be the leader of a new regime?

Mountbatten declared that this was treason. Before the end of the month King had lost his job – and a very un-British kind of coup had quietly bitten the dust.

Although the drift towards regarding the royals as mere mortals would gather pace in the years to come, the Silver Jubilee in 1977 provided an opportunity for stemming the tide through another scintillating programme of bread and circuses.

And what, after all, was there to be said against the Windsors on a personal level? Her Majesty and Prince Philip were evidently beyond reproach. The Queen Mother was in bouncing health at 77, and a bit of a character to boot. As for the four children, Charles was an eligible bachelor; Anne was married to a fellow equestrian, Captain Mark Phillips; and Andrew and Edward were personable young princes in their teens.

With hindsight, the Silver Jubilee was the last great royal occasion free of major 'ifs and buts'. Of course there were dissenters: the punk-rock group the Sex Pistols brought out a controversial version of 'God Save the Queen' which included a reference to a 'fascist regime' and climbed to the top of the charts despite the fact that the BBC refused to play it. They performed it while sailing down the Thames on Jubilee Day, and perhaps weren't surprised to find themselves arrested when they stepped ashore.

Republicans had their usual say, but the nation as a whole had a good wallow in British over-the-toppery. On 6 June (her official birthday) the Queen lit a bonfire beacon at Windsor Castle, and the light was carried onwards, Armada-style, by chains of fellow beacons across the country, besides which the locals enjoyed firework displays, barbecues and all-night dancing.

The main event was a service at St Paul's Cathedral the next day, the Queen and Prince Philip arriving in their gold coach with a million and more waving flags along the route. 'When I was 21,' she declared, 'I pledged my life to the service of our people, and I asked for God's help to make good that vow. Although that vow was made in my salad days, when I was green in judgement, I do not regret nor retract one word of it.'

The keynote of the Jubilee was 'the unity of the nation', and Elizabeth embarked on a three-month tour of the country – the most extensive of any monarch in history. There were parades and street parties (an estimated 1,200 of them) up and down the land; and Jubilee footpaths, trails, gardens and buildings, not to speak of the Jubilee Line on the London Underground (which actually opened two years later), are lasting reminders of a truly impressive knees-up.

True to form, the celebrations were not confined to Britain – and neither were the

royal visits. The Queen and Prince Philip undertook a Commonwealth tour which echoed their very first in 1953, taking in Fiji, Tonga, New Zealand, Australia and Papua New Guinea before reaching Canada via the West Indies.

JUBILEE SOAP

The TV soap opera *Coronation Street* reflected the national mood, with little Tracy Langton winning a Bonny Jubilee Baby contest and Elsie Tanner (entered against her will) reaching the final of a Glamorous Granny event.

The street's float had the theme 'Britain Through the Ages', its characters including Elizabeth I (Annie Walker), Queen Victoria (Ena Sharples), Edmund Hillary (Ken Barlow), Tenzing Norgay (Albert Tatlock) and a caveman (Eddie Yeats). Unhappily, Stan Ogden left the lorry's lights on all night so that their plans came to nothing – and he had to buy everyone drinks as a punishment.

UP THE UNION!

But did pressing the 'feelgood' button have a broader purpose than simply making the public happier about the monarchy itself? The Queen's Silver Jubilee address to Parliament that May made no bones about it.

Devolution – at its most extreme, the breaking up of the United Kingdom, with independence for Scotland and Wales – was high on the political agenda in 1977, and the Queen acknowledged 'the feeling that metropolitan government is too remote from the lives of ordinary men and women'.

She then dealt a deft body-blow: 'But I cannot forget that I was crowned Queen of the United Kingdom of Great Britain and Northern Ireland. Perhaps this Jubilee is a time to remind ourselves of the benefits which union has conferred, at home and in our international dealings, on the inhabitants of all parts of this United Kingdom.' The ensuing bunting-hung festivities are thought to have put devolution on the back burner for another 20 years.

ALL THIS – AND WIMBLEDON TOO!

It had all the trappings of a fairytale – but it was one that magically came true.

In Jubilee year, and with Wimbledon celebrating its centenary, the Queen paid her very first visit to the women's tennis final, in which England's Virginia Wade, now 31 years old, was making her 16th attempt to win the sport's greatest prize.

After she had come from behind to win 4–6, 6–3, 6–1, an ecstatic crowd chorused 'For she's a jolly good fellow'. Had she come down from cloud nine?, she was asked afterwards. 'No, I haven't,' she replied. 'I never will.'

THE TROUBLE WITH MARGARET

If the Queen needed jolting back to the reality of persistent media intrusion, she had only to consider the plight of her sister. Margaret had separated from her husband in 1976, and their divorce (the first by a royal since Henry VIII) was presumably delayed until 1978 so as not to tarnish the Jubilee celebrations.

Lively and vivacious, Margaret seems never to have been comfortable in her role as a dutiful princess, and hadn't been shy of saying so:

'My children are not royal – they just happen to have the Queen for their aunt.'

'I have as much privacy as a goldfish in a bowl.'

'I have always had a dread of becoming a passenger in life.'

She had been linked with other men within a few years of her marriage, but in 1976 the front page of the *News of the World* carried a swimsuited photograph of her on holiday in Mustique with the young landscape gardener Roddy Llewellyn (a baronet, it should be stressed, rather than a horny-handed son of toil).

Moralistic MPs called her a 'floozie' and a 'royal parasite', while the press depicted her as a predatory older woman with a toy-boy lover. (He was 17 years her junior.) Once her marriage was over she was hounded by the press, who called her 'lazy and decadent' and demanded 'Give up Roddy or quit royal duties.'

Margaret and Llewellyn remained an item for some years before he married someone else. She smoked and drank herself into ill-health, had half a lung removed, suffered partial paralysis from a stroke and ended her days needing a wheelchair. It would be the cruellest kind of republican who failed to feel some sympathy for a woman born into a life she would never have chosen.

PIONEER PAPARAZZO

Ray Bellisario, known to the press as 'the peeping Tom', was Britain's first intrusive snapper of royalty. In 1964 he took photographs of Princess Margaret in a swimsuit and they were published in the *Sunday Express*. The Palace instructed editors not to buy Bellisario's pictures – and in those more timid times many of them fell into line.

One of his coups, not published until 1998, was a photograph of the Queen walking in the grounds of Buckingham Palace in the 1960s with her uncle the Duke of Windsor, formerly Edward VIII. The official line was that he was an outcast, and that there had been no meeting.

1980S BRITAIN

1980 Unemployment reaches highest levels since 1935.

1981 Riots related to racial tension and inner-city squalor; ten IRA hunger strikers die; Rupert Murdoch buys *The Times*.

1982 *Sun* newspaper circulation reaches 4 million; Falklands War; Greenham Common women's peace camp.

1983 Seat belts become mandatory; IRA bombs in London.

1984 Miners' strike; highest percentage of workers unemployed since Great Depression; Grand Hotel, Brighton, bombed by IRA.

1985 Live Aid pop concerts; riots in Toxteth (Liverpool), Brixton, Peckham and Tottenham (London).

1986 Greater London Council abolished; outbreak of 'mad cow disease'.

1987 Church of England allows ordination of women; so-called 'hurricane' hits southern England; Channel Tunnel excavation begins.

1988 Nurses' strike; salmonella outbreak in eggs; Lockerbie airliner bombing.

1989 Hillsborough football stadium disaster; rail strike.

TELEPHOTO LENSES

During the 1980s the media frenzy intensified, to such an extent that in December 1981 the Queen's press secretary, Michael Shea, invited Fleet Street editors to the Palace, asking them to take a step back.

It was a fruitless plea. Charles had married Diana Spencer in July 1981, and the 'Queen of Hearts', as the *Sun* annointed her, was too photogenic to ignore, especially when her first pregnancy was announced. Telephoto lenses in place, the *Sun* and the *Star* followed Diana and Charles to the Bahamas and took pictures of her on holiday in a bikini.

The Queen doesn't give interviews, but we can well believe the authenticity of a comment attributed to her: 'This is the blackest day in the history of British journalism.'

Well, there were plenty more to come, and here's a taste of the kind of headlines the tabloids splashed about what they sensed was a faltering marriage:

- A PUBLIC BUST-UP!
- ARE CHARLES AND DIANA MOVING APART?
- LOVELESS MARRIAGE
- CHARLES LOSES HIS TROUSERS TO DI

AND A FEW OTHER THINGS...

All in all, it was a pretty dark decade for the royal family. Back in 1974 Princess Anne had narrowly survived a kidnap attempt, when a man later detained under the Mental Health Act had shot two police officers and a tabloid journalist (what can *he* have been doing there?) before being arrested. More scares, disasters and self-inflicted embarrassments were to follow during the 1980s:

- In June 1981 the Queen was riding down Horseguards' Parade for the start of the Trooping the Colour ceremony when 17-year-old Marcus Serjeant pointed a pistol at her and fired six times. Fortunately he had been unable to find a lethal weapon, as he had intended, and the cartridges were blanks. He was jailed under the Treason Act. The Queen appeared shaken, but soon recovered.

• In the early hours of 9 July 1982, the Queen woke to find Michael Fagan, a 32-year-old unemployed father of four, in her bedroom. (She slept alone.) It was, incredibly, Fagan's second breach of Buckingham Palace security, and when the Queen twice buzzed for help, nobody came – her armed policeman was out walking the dogs. Fagan sat on the edge of her bed chatting, and when he asked for a cigarette the Queen called for a maid to bring some in. He later spent six months in a mental hospital undergoing psychiatric evaluation.

WARTS AND ALL

If you wonder how the Queen has had the patience to sit for around 140 portraits in her lifetime, here's what she told the now disgraced TV artist and entertainer Rolf Harris: 'I'm only too happy to be sitting absolutely motionless, doing nothing.' (Well, it must make a change.)

The prize for the most attacked portrait of modern times goes to Lucian Freud. The *Sun* newspaper said he should be 'locked in the Tower', while the editor of the *British Art Journal* wrote: 'It makes her look like one of the royal corgis who has suffered a stroke.'

• Apparently having learned nothing from the *Royal Family* documentary, Prince Edward, as a would-be TV producer, persuaded Princess Anne and the Duke and Duchess of York to take part in a charity version of a once-popular slapstick series. The Queen hadn't approved the idea, and when it was screened in June 1987, with the contestants dressed in Elizabethan garb, *It's a Royal Knockout* was widely ridiculed.

• On 10 March 1988 Prince Charles almost met his death on the Swiss ski slopes at Klosters. An avalanche swept down on the prince and his party, killing one of his closest friends, Major Hugh Lindsay, and badly injuring another of the party, Patti Palmer-Tomkinson. (The major's wife, Sarah, who worked in the Buckingham Palace press office, was six months pregnant.) Once the danger had passed, Charles, their guide and a police officer raced back to dig in the snow with their bare hands to reach the victims.

THE COMMON TOUCH

Although, mercifully, she could not know it, the Queen had an even worse decade ahead of her. In the meantime, whatever her view of the changing world about her, she made a practised fist of keeping in touch with the day-to-day life of her ordinary subjects.

She even began to *sound* more like them. A study by Australian academics, who listened to recordings of the Queen's Christmas broadcasts from the 1950s to the 1980s, discovered that her vowels had shifted from their original upper-class register to sounds something like those of standard southern British (SSB). In those early postwar years her pronunciation of 'had' almost rhymed with 'bed', while 'home' was 'hame'.

One of her own homes, Windsor Castle, had long been open to the public, but soon (albeit driven by necessity) she would be inviting the common herd into Buckingham Palace too. This, it should be added, would be at times when Her Majesty was far away. After all, she did have rather a lot of homes to choose from...

ROYAL RESIDENCES

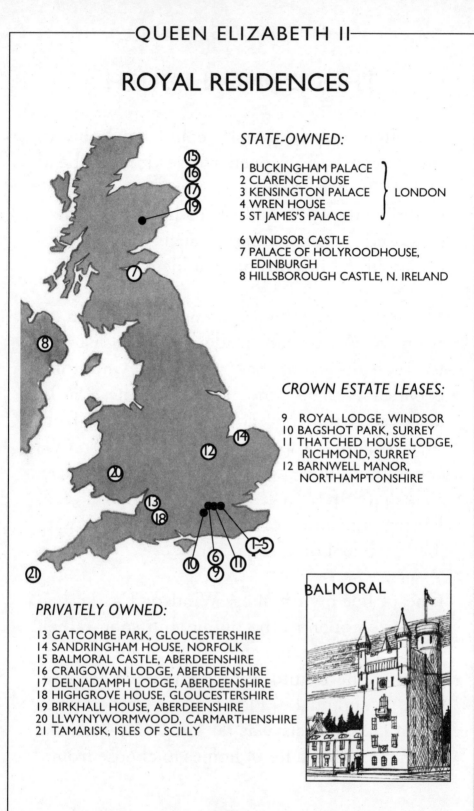

STATE-OWNED:

1 BUCKINGHAM PALACE
2 CLARENCE HOUSE
3 KENSINGTON PALACE ⎫ LONDON
4 WREN HOUSE
5 ST JAMES'S PALACE ⎭

6 WINDSOR CASTLE
7 PALACE OF HOLYROODHOUSE, EDINBURGH
8 HILLSBOROUGH CASTLE, N. IRELAND

CROWN ESTATE LEASES:

9 ROYAL LODGE, WINDSOR
10 BAGSHOT PARK, SURREY
11 THATCHED HOUSE LODGE, RICHMOND, SURREY
12 BARNWELL MANOR, NORTHAMPTONSHIRE

PRIVATELY OWNED:

13 GATCOMBE PARK, GLOUCESTERSHIRE
14 SANDRINGHAM HOUSE, NORFOLK
15 BALMORAL CASTLE, ABERDEENSHIRE
16 CRAIGOWAN LODGE, ABERDEENSHIRE
17 DELNADAMPH LODGE, ABERDEENSHIRE
18 HIGHGROVE HOUSE, GLOUCESTERSHIRE
19 BIRKHALL HOUSE, ABERDEENSHIRE
20 LLWYNYWORMWOOD, CARMARTHENSHIRE
21 TAMARISK, ISLES OF SCILLY

BALMORAL

WHERE THE OTHER HALF LIVES

The Queen may not be short of a bob or two (there's no general agreement about the true size of her personal fortune), but she owns rather fewer grand properties than you might imagine – and not a single palace.

Back in 1760 George III ran into money troubles, and his solution was to do a deal with Parliament, handing over all income from land owned by the Crown in return for a 'Civil List' annuity which paid for his family's upkeep and his royal duties. With tweaks, this system has persisted ever since.

THE CROWN ESTATE

In Britain's constitutional democracy the word 'Crown' rather confusingly denotes the State. The vast holdings of the Crown Estate (a commercially run corporation) raise some £190 million a year for the Treasury.

What it owns:

- Windsor Great Park, Regent's Park in London and almost all of Regent Street

- a UK-wide urban portfolio including shops, offices, retail and business parks, industrial sites and residential properties

- about a thousand listed buildings, 37 per cent of them Grade 1

- 358 acres (145 ha) of agricultural land.

- more than half of the UK's foreshore and tidal riverbeds, and almost all of the seabed within the 12 nautical mile (22.25 km) limit – and all whales and sturgeons washed ashore

- rights to all naturally occurring gold and silver – the Mines Royal.

What it leases to the royals:

- Royal Lodge Windsor (Duke of York)

- Bagshot Park, Surrey (the Wessexes)

- Thatched House Lodge, Richmond, Surrey (Princess Alexandra)

- Barnwell Manor, Northamptonshire (the Gloucesters).

Since 2001 the Crown Estate has made an annual Civil List payment of £7.9 million to the Queen for the running of her royal household, while the revenues of the well-endowed Duchy of Lancaster provide most of her personal income. (The Duchy of Cornwall similarly funds Prince Charles.)

For the record, on 1st April 2012 the Civil List was replaced by a 'Sovereign Support Grant' linked to a portion of the Crown Estate revenue – although this didn't, of course, put an end to the long-running debate about whether the British monarchy earns its keep.

A TAXING PROBLEM

When the Queen Mother died in 2002 she left a fortune of around £50 million to the Queen – who didn't have to pay a penny in inheritance tax. This special deal had been agreed in 1993, the Conservative prime minister John Major accepting the view that the Queen shouldn't have her wealth eroded, but should be able to 'live in a way commensurate with the dignity of a head of State'. After all, if she had to pay something like £20 million in inheritance tax, mightn't she be reduced to selling Balmoral or Sandringham to keep her head above water?

With a masterly political sleight of hand, however, Major came away with a sop to those who criticised this astounding generosity: the Queen had, for the very first time, voluntarily agreed to pay income tax. (Not surprisingly, the size of the taxable amount would be hidden from prying eyes.)

Y BWTHYN BACH

This is the name (meaning 'The Little House') of a miniature thatched cottage presented to the young princesses Elizabeth and Margaret as a gift from the people of Wales in 1932.

Transported by lorry from the Principality to the grounds of Royal Lodge, Windsor, it had to make the journey twice: on the first occasion there was an accident and it caught fire.

Small though it may be – adults have to stoop to enter – it's supplied with hot and cold running water, electricity and a telephone. The surrounding hedges are scaled down to size.

A HOME OF ONE'S OWN

Several large houses are privately owned by members of the royal family.

The Queen:

- Sandringham House, Norfolk
- Balmoral Castle, Aberdeen
- Craigowan Lodge, Aberdeenshire
- Delnadamph Lodge, Aberdeenshire

Prince Charles:

- Highgrove House, Gloucestershire
- Birkhall House, Balmoral
- Llwynywormwood, Carmarthenshire
- Tamarisk, Isles of Scilly

The Princess Royal:

- Gatcombe Park, Gloucestershire

Prince Charles, too, would be taxed on his income. He had previously paid the Treasury 25 per cent of Duchy of Cornwall profits – in future he would pay the current rate of income tax (40 per cent in 1993), but only after deductions for such business outgoings as his 100-plus staff. The calculation was that he'd be no worse off at the end of the day, but an important principle had been established.

A LAW UNTO THEMSELVES

The royal palaces have special legal privileges, including some exemptions from workaday health and safety regulations.

Technically a royal residence, the Palace of Westminster – or the Houses of Parliament to you and me – doesn't need a licence to sell alcohol in its many bars, and it's excused tax on drink, too. Since some of its 20 bars never close while the House is sitting, the temptation for members to quaff the cheap wine and beer in liberal quantities must be extreme.

Other facilities for the MPs range from a gym and a hair salon to a rifle range.

MARBLE HALLS

It's time for a checklist of the castles, palaces and stately homes which the State provides, free of charge, for the royals to live in.

London:

- Buckingham Palace (the Queen, Prince Andrew, the Wessexes)

- St James's Palace, Pall Mall (Princess Royal, Princess Alexandra)

- Clarence House, St James's Palace (the Prince of Wales, Princes William and Harry)

- Kensington Palace (the Gloucesters, Prince and Princess Michael of Kent)

- Wren House, Kensington Palace (the Kents)

Berkshire:

- Windsor Castle (various)

Edinburgh:

- Palace of Holyroodhouse (various)

Northern Ireland:

- Hillsborough Castle (various).

A YEAR IN THE LIFE

The Queen travels far and wide on her visits, as we've seen, but there is an established pattern to her movements.

- **Buckingham Palace:** Monday to Friday. (She spends an average of three hours every day 'doing the boxes' – reading State papers.)

- **Windsor Castle:** most weekends; a month at Easter, and a week in June for Royal Ascot.

- **Palace of Holyroodhouse:** Holyrood week in July, and whenever she is carrying out official duties in Scotland.

- **Sandringham House:** from Christmas until February.

- **Balmoral Castle:** August and September.

THE SCOTTISH CONNECTION

The royal family's fondness for Scotland owes something to a blood relationship: the Queen Mother, brought up in Glamis Castle, was the daughter of the Scottish Earl of Strathmore and his English countess.

Balmoral, however, was bought by Queen Victoria and Prince Albert after they fell in love with the area on a visit two years after their wedding. They acquired the estate in 1848, built a new castle ('My dear paradise in the Highlands', Victoria called it) and demolished the old one.

HEARTH AND HOME

And how do the royals relax away from the public gaze? We know rather more than they would like, thanks to Ryan Parry, a graduate trainee reporter with the *Daily Mirror*, who in 1993 spent two months 'under cover' as a footman liveried in scarlet and gold braid at Windsor Castle and Buckingham Palace.

Parry's purported aim was to demonstrate security failings (he'd produced fake ID to get the job), but the public was more interested in the day-to-day minutiae of life with the Windsors. Buckingham Palace swiftly sued the newspaper and was granted £25,000 towards the Queen's legal costs and an injunction to prevent further revelations, while Parry won the Scoop of the Year award.

He found pomp and circumstance to be markedly (perhaps reassuringly) lacking:

- At the breakfast table the Queen's cornflakes and porridge were kept in plastic Tupperware boxes. She liked her toast lightly spread with marmalade, and would bury her head in the *Racing Post* while Philip listened to a small and ageing Roberts transistor radio.

- The Queen's television preferences included *East Enders*, *The Bill* and Sky One's *Kirsty's Home Videos* (useful for keeping in touch with her subjects?), while she also enjoyed video re-runs of the racing.

- Edward and Sophie, the earl and countess of Wessex, littered their bed with furry bears and dogs.

- Prince Andrew's sitting room was lined with red and pink flock wallpaper, and a pillow bore the motto 'Eat, drink and remarry'.

The Palace found published photographs of the royal bedrooms particularly disquieting, and these were ordered to be destroyed.

Parry also passed a few judgements on the personalities he encountered:

- *Prince Andrew:* Grumpy and foul-mouthed when the staff woke him up in the morning. He amused himself by hiding a stuffed monkey puppet in odd places around the Palace.

- *The Princess Royal:* Abrupt but fair.

- *The Countess of Wessex:* Kind.

BROUGHT TO BOOK

The writer Alan Bennett has some gentle fun with the monarch's supposed lack of literary interests in his novella *The Uncommon Reader*.

In his fantasy, the Queen stumbles across a mobile library in the Palace grounds, takes out a book so as not to offend the staff – and finds herself completely hooked.

Before long, as her passion grows, she is hiding novels under her cushions to sneak a furtive read whenever possible, and her courtiers worry that she is neglecting her royal duties. But, she tells herself, she is a 'doing' person. Surely she should start to *write* . . .

ALL THE QUEEN'S HORSES
(AND A FEW OTHER CREATURES, TOO)

Were she not destined to be Queen, the 12-year-old Elizabeth told Crawfie somewhat wistfully, she would have liked to be 'a lady living in the country with lots of horses and dogs'.

Well, in the end she got her way, at least some of the time…

HORSES

The Queen on horseback in a headscarf (what a bad example!) is a familiar holiday picture at Sandringham, Windsor or Balmoral. A first-class horsewoman, she is also a breeder, with some 25 thoroughbreds in training each year.

Her racing colours are purple body with gold braid; scarlet sleeves; and black velvet cap with a gold fringe – and horses from the royal studs have won almost every major race in Britain over the years.

Her favourite Trooping the Colour horse was the black mare Burmese (1962–1990), given to her by the Royal Canadian Mounted Police.

DOGS

Corgis may be her favourites – she took one with her on her honeymoon, and has had more than 30 during her reign – but the Queen also breeds labradors and cocker spaniels at Sandringham. When one of her corgis was mated with Princess Margaret's dachshund Pipkin, the offspring was declared to be a 'dorgi', and the Queen now has several of them.

Not everyone has treated Her Majesty's canines with respect. In 1999 one of her footmen was demoted after it emerged that he had entertained other staff members by adding whisky and gin to the corgis' food and water, making them tipsy.

RACING PIGEONS

The royal family was first given racing pigeons by King Leopold II of Belgium in 1886, and the Queen is an enthusiast. One of her birds took part in the Pau International race in 1990, coming first in its section, and was subsequently named Sandringham Lightning. The Queen is patron of several racing societies, including the Royal Pigeon Racing Association.

FURTHER REVELATIONS

The royal butler Paul Burrell (whom we shall meet again later on) scandalised Buckingham Palace by publishing his memoirs. Here are a few of his claims about life 'below stairs':

- Housemaids weren't allowed to use vacuum cleaners before 9.00 a.m. in case they disturbed the royal family.

- The class system was 'straight from the decks of the *Titanic'*, with the junior staff eating in a workplace-style canteen while the most senior ate food off fine china plates and drank wine from the royal cellars.

- Staff at the lower end were paid a pittance, and stringent house rules made a social life outside almost impossible.

- Some turned to drink: 'Footmen became expert at siphoning off gin every day from crystal decanters and pouring sneaky supplies into chrome kettles.'

- Several attempted suicide, while others were pensioned off suffering from mental breakdowns.

UP TO THE ELBOWS

Even the former prime minister Tony Blair went into royal 'fancy that' mode in his memoirs, *A Journey*. He seemed amazed that the Queen should help tidy up after a family barbecue at Balmoral and that the royal family should take it in turns to wash up.

'You think I'm joking, but I'm not,' he wrote. 'They put the gloves on and stick their hands in the sink.'

Another prime minister, Margaret Thatcher, was apparently sufficiently mortified to see Her Majesty doing anything so humble with her bare hands that she tried to take over the job herself (she was politely rebuffed), and then – the story is too good not to be believed – thoughtfully sent her a pair of rubber gloves as a present the following Christmas.

BUCKINGHAM PALACE

If you know the fantastical pseudo- Indian/ Chinese Royal Pavilion created by the Prince Regent and his architect John Nash in Brighton, you may be surprised to learn that the pair were also responsible for the French-neoclassical pile which is Buckingham Palace.

Originally Buckingham House, it was bought in 1761 by George III as a comfortable family home for Queen Charlotte, and 14 of their 15 children were born there. As soon as his father died in 1830, the extravagant 'Prinny' (now George IV) began reconstructing the building, and it wasn't long before he decided that it should become a veritable palace.

The north and south wings were demolished and rebuilt on a larger scale, the centrepiece of its enlarged courtyard being the Marble Arch, to commemorate the British victories at Trafalgar and Waterloo.

As anyone might have predicted, the costs escalated phenomenally – to the massive sum for those days of half a million pounds –

and poor Nash lost his job because of the extravagance.

Queen Victoria was the first monarch to live in the new palace, and it still wasn't big enough for her and her growing family. The Marble Arch was moved to the northeast corner of Hyde Park so that a new wing could be created, and the cost was partially defrayed by selling off the Royal Pavilion.

THANK YOU, MA'AM

The Queen provides all her staff with gifts at Christmas, and — continuing a custom begun by George V — has distributed around 90,000 Christmas puddings over the years. She also stages an end-of-year drinks party for her staff in the state rooms at Buckingham Palace.

During her summer stay at Balmoral she thanks her *ghillies* (Scottish servants) and other staff by holding the Ghillies' Ball. Members of the local community are invited, and the Queen and Prince Philip begin the evening by joining three other couples in an eightsome reel.

'BUCK HOUSE' FACTS AND FIGURES

- The building measures 108 m (355 ft) across the front by 120 m (394 ft) deep, including its central quad.

- It has 775 rooms, including 19 state rooms, 52 royal and guest bedrooms, 188 staff bedrooms, 92 offices and 78 bathrooms.

- The ballroom, opened in 1856 to celebrate the end of the Crimean War, was the largest room in London at the time: 36.6 m (120 ft) long by 18 m (59 ft) wide and 13.5 m (44 ft) high. State banquets are held here today, attended by up to 1,500 guests.

- More than 50,000 people visit each year, as guests at banquets, lunches, dinners, receptions and royal garden parties.

- The forecourt, where Changing the Guard takes place, was formed in 1911, and a few years later the façade of the building was completely refaced with Portland stone.

- After a German bomb hit the Palace in September 1940, the Queen Mother (then Queen Elizabeth) took comfort from the fact that the royals were suffering alongside their fellow Londoners. 'Now we can look the East End in the face,' she said.

TEN PALACE INTERLOPERS

We've already (page 99) recounted the story of Michael Fagan's breaking into the Queen's bedroom. Here are ten more Palace incursions:

1989 Michael Crook tries to talk to the Queen by the royal stables.

1990 Stephen Goulding breaks into the grounds, claiming to be Prince Andrew.

1993 Anti-nuclear protesters scale the walls and stage a sit-down on the lawn.

1994 James Miller circles the Palace in a paraglider before landing on the roof and exposing himself.

1995 Student John Gillard rams the gates with his car at 50 mph.

1997 An absconding mental patient wanders around the grounds.

2000 Author Brett De La Mare paraglides into the forecourt as a publicity stunt.

2003 A 27-year-old man is arrested in the grounds after climbing a wall.

2004 Fathers 4 Justice campaigner Jason Hatch, dressed as Batman, unfurls a banner on the balcony.

2009 Undercover reporters posing as Middle Eastern businessmen are let into the grounds by a royal chauffeur.

A BOTTLE OR TWO

Staging some 800 events a year, the Palace gets through a prodigious amount of wine and spirits. The yeoman of the cellar, his deputy and an under-butler look after a store reputedly worth £2 million in several large rooms off a labyrinth of underground corridors.

Since 2007 these have been cooled by water drawn from a borehole in the grounds, and a cold-air curtain keeps the temperature at 10–12^{0}C (50–55.5^{0}F). The wines (selected at blind tastings by a committee of experts) are bought when young and allowed to mature – for at least 12 years, in the case of claret.

APPARITIONS

Most ancient buildings attract ghostly legends. The story goes that a medieval priory occupied the land on which the Palace now stands, and that every Christmas Day a chained monk makes a fleeting appearance in the grounds.

Another reported apparition relates to a known tragedy. Edward VII's private secretary, Major John Gwynne, became involved in a divorce scandal which ruined his reputation. Unable to cope with the disgrace, he took a pistol into his office and blew his brains out. Staff have reported hearing a phantom shot coming from the room.

THE WRONG KIND OF MULBERRY

Lancelot 'Capability' Brown landscaped the Buckingham Palace grounds, which cover 42 acres (17 hectares), encompass 2½ miles (4 km) of gravel paths and are cared for by a team of eight full-time gardeners. Here you'll find not only lawns, flowerbeds, trees and a large lake, but a helicopter pad, a pitch-and-putt course installed for Prince Andrew, and a tennis court which has been used by Björn Borg, John McEnroe and Steffi Graf.

In the southeast corner there's also a single mulberry tree surviving from the time when James I imported 100,000 into the country with the idea of launching a home-grown silk industry. Alas, he should have purchased white mulberries, but unhappily introduced the black variety instead – and it proved useless.

WINDSOR CASTLE

The Queen's favourite bolt-hole is a building described variously as the longest-occupied palace in Europe and the oldest and largest occupied castle in the world.

Originally built by William the Conqueror after 1066 to defend strategically important land by the Thames, it was expanded by various monarchs over the centuries. Charles II, whose father had been imprisoned there by Parliamentary forces in the Civil War, created a set of extravagant baroque interiors. George III and George IV spent even more on the magnificent state apartments with their gothic, baroque and rococo furnishings.

- The castle and its grounds cover 13 acres (5 hectares); 500 people live and work there.

- Its centrepiece is the Middle Ward – a bailey (enclosure) formed around the motte (artificial hill) at its centre. This is topped by the tower, or keep.

- The Upper Ward is flanked by the magnificent state apartments and the private royal quarters.

- The Lower Ward, largely redesigned in the Victorian period, contains various buildings associated with the Order of the Garter. The most important, and largest, of them is St George's Chapel, which dates from the late 15th century and is the burial place of ten monarchs.

- The Home Park, to the east of the castle, includes parkland and two working farms. It adjoins the northern edge of Windsor Great Park, which occupies 4,800 acres (1,900 hectares) and includes some of the oldest broadleaved woodlands in Europe.

QUEEN MARY'S DOLLS' HOUSE

Despite the gilded richness on display throughout the castle, the highlight for some visitors is the 1:12 scale dolls' house made for Queen Mary in the 1920s.

The famous architect Sir Edwin Lutyens designed it, and leading artists and craftsmen of the time were brought in to create a collection of miniature items which actually work – including light fittings and a flushable lavatory. Writers such as Sir Arthur Conan Doyle, Thomas Hardy and Rudyard Kipling wrote special books which were bound in scale size, while painters provided tiny pictures.

UP IN FLAMES

At 11.33 on the morning of 20 November 1992, a spotlight ignited a curtain in the Queen's private chapel at Windsor – and within minutes a major conflagration had taken hold. By 12.20 it had spread to St George's Hall, the largest of the state apartments, and was being tackled by all of 225 firemen using 39 appliances – the biggest turnout in Greater London for decades.

The teams worked through the night as flames spread through the roof voids. Fifteen hours later, when the fire was at last brought under control, nine of the principal state rooms had been completely destroyed and another hundred severely damaged. Some areas which were spared the worst of the heat and smoke had been wrecked by 1.5 million gallons (6.8 million litres) of hosed water.
A burning question

WINDSOR CASTLE TRIVIA

- It has more than 450 manually wound clocks.

- The royal librarian is the custodian of 300,000 books, prints and works of art.

- A 'fendersmith' is employed to look after the 300-plus fireplaces — and the 2006 incumbent, Gary Jones, did his job so well that he was awarded the Royal Victorian Medal (Silver) in the New Year's Honours List.

- The bullet which killed Admiral Lord Nelson at Trafalgar is on display in the Grand Vestibule.

Nobody doubted that Windsor Castle had to be made good again, but State buildings were routinely not insured — and the cost of the repairs would turn out to be almost £40 million. So who should pay?

The Queen's decision in February 1993 to sign up for income tax (see pages 105–106) was a direct consequence of the fire which had swept through her weekend home less than three months earlier. And the opening up of Buckingham Palace that same year followed from it, too.

Why? Because, with support for the monarchy at a miserably low ebb, several national newspapers had trumpeted the idea that the Queen should pay for the Windsor Castle repairs out of her own private income.

This, in turn, stimulated a wider debate. What about all those lesser, 'fringe' royals who were paid out of the Exchequer's funds – did they really offer a decent return on the considerable outlay? Was the royal family little more than a vainglorious drain on the nation's resources?

With the Conservative government under intense pressure in the House of Commons, a deal was reached to head off a constitutional crisis. The Queen now agreed to:

• pay income tax from the following April

• restrict those members of the royal family being paid from the public purse to just herself, the Duke of Edinburgh and the Queen Mother (she would fund the rest from her own income)

- meet 70 per cent of the cost of the Windsor repair work herself

- open up Buckingham Palace to the public in order to generate extra funds to pay for the restoration. (At the same time new charges would be introduced for public access to the parkland surrounding Windsor Castle.)

So it was that for eight weeks during the summer of 1993 people queued outside the Palace in their hundreds in order to take a step inside for the very first time – and to raise (at £8 a head) more than £2 million towards the restoration.

Would this be enough to silence the vociferous critics of the Queen and her family?

She had to hope so. After all, by her own acknowledgement she had just endured the very worst year of her reign…

ELIZABETH'S HEIRS

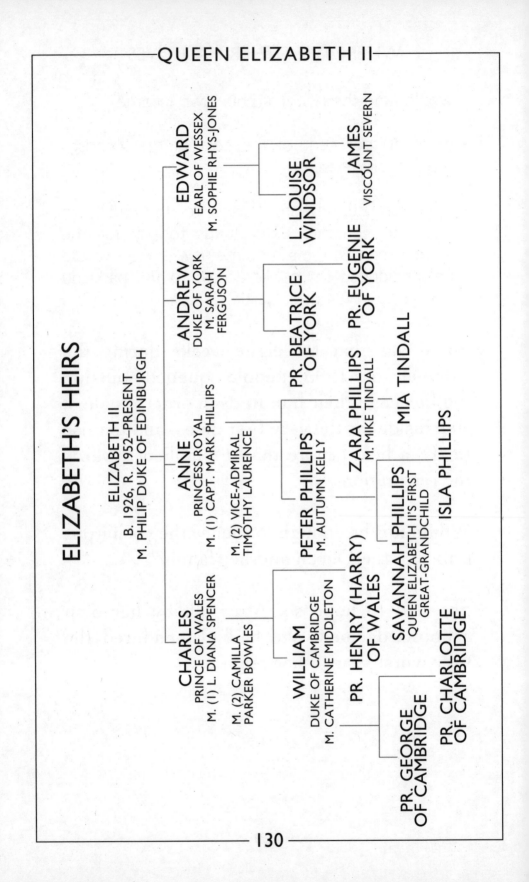

ELIZABETH II
B. 1926, R. 1952–PRESENT
M. PHILIP DUKE OF EDINBURGH

CHARLES
PRINCE OF WALES
M. (1) L. DIANA SPENCER

M. (2) CAMILLA
PARKER BOWLES

ANNE
PRINCESS ROYAL
M. (1) CAPT. MARK PHILLIPS

M. (2) VICE-ADMIRAL
TIMOTHY LAURENCE

ANDREW
DUKE OF YORK
M. SARAH
FERGUSON

EDWARD
EARL OF WESSEX
M. SOPHIE RHYS-JONES

WILLIAM
DUKE OF CAMBRIDGE
M. CATHERINE MIDDLETON

PR. HENRY (HARRY)
OF WALES

PETER PHILLIPS
M. AUTUMN KELLY

ZARA PHILLIPS
M. MIKE TINDALL

PR. BEATRICE
OF YORK

PR. EUGENIE
OF YORK

L. LOUISE
WINDSOR

JAMES
VISCOUNT SEVERN

PR. GEORGE
OF CAMBRIDGE

PR. CHARLOTTE
OF CAMBRIDGE

SAVANNAH PHILLIPS
QUEEN ELIZABETH II'S FIRST
GREAT-GRANDCHILD

ISLA PHILLIPS

MIA TINDALL

I t was in a speech at London's Guildhall to mark her 40 years on the throne that she said it: '1992 is not a year on which I shall look back with undiluted pleasure. In the words of one of my more sympathetic correspondents, it has turned out to be an *Annus Horribilis*.'

Windsor Castle had burst into flames only days before, but that was not all. During this 'horrible year' the marriages of three of the Queen's four children had come to grief amid a series of lurid media exposés.

A CALL FOR UNDERSTANDING

*An extract from the Queen's Guildhall speech,
24 November 1992*

'I sometimes wonder how future generations will judge the events of this tumultuous year. I dare say that history will take a slightly more moderate view than that of some contemporary commentators.

'Distance is well known to lend enchantment . . . but it can also lend an extra dimension to judgement, giving it a leavening of moderation and compassion – even of wisdom – that is sometimes lacking in the reactions of those whose task it is in life to offer instant opinions on all things great and small.

'There can be no doubt, of course, that criticism is good for people and institutions that are part of public life. No institution – City, Monarchy, whatever – should expect to be free from the scrutiny of those who give it their loyalty and support, not to mention those who don't.

'But we are all part of the same fabric of our national society and that scrutiny, by one part of another, can be just as effective if it is made with a touch of gentleness, good humour and understanding.'

This short speech to a gathering of City of London notables was as harsh a coded condemnation of her tormentors as it was possible to make without declaring outright war on them – and, needless to say, it fell upon deaf ears.

The *Sun* even went so far as to leak the text of the Queen's Christmas Day broadcast a few weeks later – an openly defiant act to which the Palace responded by banning the paper's photographer from snapping the royal family at church on Christmas Day. Touché!

'Gentleness, good humour and understanding'? The Queen was about to endure the continued ransacking of her family's seamier secrets, the media taking a no-holds-barred approach to their pursuit of an ever more vulnerable prey. Phone-tapping, intrusive photography, payments for intimate behind-the-scenes revelations – nothing seemed to be off limits.

What's more, some of the royals now became adroit at exploiting newspaper and television coverage themselves, so losing any moral advantage they might otherwise have claimed.

Here are a few of the family 'lowlights' from that year of (dis)grace, 1992:

- March: Prince Andrew and Sarah Ferguson announce plans to separate.
- April: Princess Anne and Mark Phillips divorce on the grounds of his adultery.
- November: Windsor Castle is badly damaged by fire.
- December: Charles and Diana formally announce their decision to separate.

A PALACE BUST-UP

Sports headlines are often witty, and one of the best-remembered appeared above a report of a tempestuous football match at Selhurst Park, the Crystal Palace ground. After the home forward Gerry Queen was sent off for violent conduct, the tongue-in-cheek headline read:

QUEEN IN BRAWL AT PALACE

That was in the 1970s. Had the incident occurred in the 1990s an unsuspecting reader might well have been fooled into believing the worst – if only for a second or two.

1990s BRITAIN

1990 Poll tax riots; IRA bomb kills Eastbourne Conservative MP Ian Gow.

1991 Cannon Street rail crash; IRA bombs at Paddington and Victoria stations; poll tax abolished.

1992 Premier League founded; Church of England votes to allow women priests.

1993 James Bulger and Stephen Lawrence murdered; BNP wins first council seat.

1994 Sunday trading legalised; opening of Channel Tunnel.

1995 Race riots in Bradford; Nick Leeson jailed for Barings Bank rogue trading.

1996 First genetically modified foods on sale; IRA bombs London Docklands and Manchester city centre; Dunblane massacre.

1997 Sports sponsorship by tobacco firms to be banned; first Harry Potter book published; Hong Kong handed over to China.

1998 Good Friday Agreement between UK and Irish governments; Human Rights Act passed.

1999 Millennium Stadium opens in Wales; Ladbroke Grove rail crash.

FERGIE EXPOSED

The flavour of the tabloids' intrusion into royal affairs – salacious, with a liberal dose of coarse humour – is captured by the *Daily Mirror*'s 'exclusive' coverage of Sarah Ferguson's holiday that August with the American financial manager John Bryan.

A photographer had managed to get shots of a topless 'Fergie' on a sunbed, with Bryan perhaps kissing her foot – although 'sucking her toe' was the phrase that stuck in the popular imagination. Many more photographs were splashed not only on the front page but on spread after spread inside, showing many an exposed area of the duchess's anatomy.

What was a poor sports editor to do when faced with this competition? Manchester United, with their own Ferguson in charge, had just begun the inaugural Premier League season with two defeats and a draw, and so (briefly) were the lowest-placed team in the league. The headline now seems inevitable:

FERGIE'S BOTTOM!

BEYOND THE PALE

By all accounts the Duke of Edinburgh was fond of his brash, red-haired daughter-in-law, but the Queen was 'not amused'. News of the scandal broke while the family were relaxing at Balmoral – Fergie among them – and she was promptly forced to pack her bags and leave. She was never to be part of their inner circle again.

Fergie had been popular with the public for introducing a bit of down-to-earth vulgarity to the stuffy royal circle. Once she had fallen from grace, though, this noisy, cheerful side of her personality was precisely what the haughty aristocratic traditionalists condemned her for: she had never shown proper restraint.

Although she maintained a good relationship with Andrew after their divorce, and they shared the care of their two daughters, the duchess was increasingly sniped at by the media for being greedy, selfish and out of control – and she often, it has to be said, presented her persecutors with all the ammunition they needed.

ROYAL SOAP

Princess Anne usually demonstrated how the royals liked things done (although engagingly humorous at times, she had a reputation for being cool and disdainful), but even she had succumbed to the lure of Michael Parkinson's TV chat-show during the 1980s, appearing with her husband at a time when insiders knew full well that their marriage was on the rocks.

Of course they were asked the inevitable question about the 'rumours', eliciting a nervous and unconvincing exchange:

Anne: 'What are we doing here?'

Phillips: 'Should we leave by different doors?'

Anne: 'We *came* in the same car.'

For the British public, of course, divorce itself no longer carried a social stigma. Whereas back in 1952 fewer than 34,000 couples had cut the marital knot, the 1992 figure was 160,000. Didn't the Queen's year of troubles simply make her appear, sympathetically, just like the rest of us with all our human frailties?

Perhaps. But the royals had become a grand soap opera. Those frailties were far more gripping than anything else in their lives – and the more outrageous the better, thank you!

AN EXPENSIVE PAINT JOB

'Air Miles Andy,' some called him – a prince who worked for nothing as a British trade ambassador around the world, but who time and again offended his hosts with blunt and inconsiderate remarks.

An incident in Los Angeles, when at least he had the excuse of relative youth, revealed his yobbish streak. Meeting a group of reporters, he primed a paint spraygun and fired it all over them and their expensive cameras – later claiming that it had been an accident.

The Queen was obliged to pay several thousand pounds in damages.

STRAIGHT TALKING

Prince Edward, the youngest of the Queen's brood, had got off to a bad start by resigning his commission in the Royal Marines only four months after joining up. A taste of military life was *de rigueur* for royal males, but Edward soon discovered that he just wasn't suited to the rigours of a commando training course – and found himself vilified by the popular papers as a pathetic, ineffectual wimp.

It didn't help that his alternative choice of career was the theatre, seen by the popular press as a rather effete profession. The red-top papers, conservative as ever, continued to treat it as something shameful when a man in the public eye was felt to be acting in a less than manly way.

Edward felt the need to publicly deny the media insinuations by making an 'I'm not gay' declaration to the *Daily Mirror* in 1990, but some of the doubters failed to be persuaded even by his marriage to the PR consultant Sophie Rhys-Jones in 1999. Two years later an interview by the *News of the World* about the possibility of her undergoing IVF fertility treatment was headlined 'MY EDWARD'S NOT GAY'.

Discussing these details of her personal life, though par for the course in the 1990s, wouldn't have been necessary but for an embarrassing lack of judgement involving the *News of the World*'s notorious investigative undercover reporter Mazher Mahmood.

A KING IN WAITING?

In 1994, two years after winning 8 per cent of the votes in their country's first post-Soviet elections, the leaders of the Independent Royalist Party of Estonia wrote to Prince Edward asking him to be their king should they ever come to power. Their letter expressed admiration for the prince and for 'Britain, its monarchy, democracy and culture'.

It should be added that the party, now extinct, was a protest movement which used humour as a weapon (holding an eating strike instead of a hunger strike, for example) – and there's no record of Edward's reply, if he ever made one.

Unlikely as it seems, Mahmood time and again managed to entice indiscretions from celebrities while disguised as a Saudi sheikh – white jalaba, flowing robe, headdress, Rolex watch, hubble-bubble pipe and a Ferrari or helicopter thrown in if necessary.

Rhys-Jones not only made disparaging remarks to him about members of the British government, but gave the impression that she was using her royal status to win new clients. It was to prevent the publication of this explosive material that she had agreed to the IVF interview, but this was to do her no good – her comments appeared in the *Mail on Sunday* in any case.

The following year the couple announced that they were both giving up their business interests to concentrate on their royal duties. They then produced two children and were no longer much of a story. The allegedly gay prince had, ironically, proved to be the only one of the Queen's offspring to have achieved a happy first marriage.

MAHMOOD STRIKES AGAIN

Princess Michael of Kent was another royal entrapped by the 'fake sheikh'. She entertained him when trying to sell her £6 million house in the Cotswolds.

Although the *News of the World* called her remarks 'treachery', they were in truth little more than tittle-tattle. More entertaining were her claim that she could secure a white tiger for the sheikh (she sent pictures of herself feeding cubs), and her put-down of Prince Charles over food marketed under his Duchy Originals label: 'He doesn't make it himself. He's got the factories – it's just got his name on it.'

NOT LOVE, ACTUALLY

But the soap to end all soaps was the long-running drama of the Charles and Diana marriage and its technicolour aftermath. Here a doomed relationship unravelled in all its pain and despair, year after emotion-draining year, before the full gaze of a morbidly fascinated public – until the very monarchy came under threat and the Queen herself was forced to intervene.

It's not only with hindsight that their gilded St Paul's Cathedral wedding in the high summer of 1981 appears a sham. Many knew about its fatal flaw at the time, including a media which shamelessly played up the 'fairytale' fantasy of the 32-year-old heir to the throne marrying a pretty and innocent 20-year-old from a family even higher in the aristocratic pecking order than the Windsors themselves.

And the public? Most knew little of the background story, but millions had seen a television interview with the engaged couple, and the revealing answers when asked whether they were in love:

Diana (with a coy smile): 'Of course!'

Charles (guardedly): 'Whatever "love" means.'

The nervous Diana giggled, but surely in that moment she must have suspected the worst – that this was the usual aristocratic set-up in which the man chooses the woman best suited to provide him with an heir, not a woman to cherish.

That fatal flaw is simply expressed: Charles had been in love (whatever that was) with Camilla Parker Bowles for years; he was still in love with her now; and their affair would continue throughout his married life. Diana had no chance.

During the first few years of the marriage there were countless press stories about Diana's unhappiness and about the fact that the couple were spending long periods apart. (The Palace, of course, denied any rift.)

THE CAMILLA FILE

Born Camilla Shand in 1947, the daughter of an army officer, she first met Charles in 1970 at a polo match – she was as keen an aficionado of country pursuits as he was.

The Palace thought her an unsuitable match for the future king, and in 1972 Charles left for military duty overseas without asking her to wait for him. The following year she married Andrew Parker Bowles, a former flame of Princess Anne.

Her relationship with the prince resumed a few years later – and never ended. She and Parker Bowles divorced in 1995.

PILING ON THE AGONY

By the beginning of that *Annus Horribilis*, 1992, it was obvious that the stories were true, and by now Diana herself was fashioning a public role for herself as the betrayed wife. That February, on an official state visit to India with Charles, she posed alone for the cameras on a bench in front of the Taj Mahal, that 'epitome of love'. The newspapers were delighted to be so blatantly manipulated.

From now on the revelations intensified, the public being fed a diet of the most intimate, often sordid, details by a shameless, lip-smacking media.

• **March:** Lady Colin Campbell publishes her book *The Real Diana*, serialised in the *Sunday Mirror*, which explores Diana's relationship with four men.

• **May:** Andrew Morton's more devastating *Diana: Her True Story* is published, and is serialised the following month in the *Sunday Times*. Although the Palace denies that Diana co-operated with Morton, it later transpires that she did. The book details her bulimia, her suicide attempts and the insensitivity of Charles and other members of his family.

• **June:** The Palace asks the Press Complaints Commission to intervene, saying that 'The most recent intrusive and speculative treatment by sections of the press, and indeed by broadcasters, of the marriage of the Prince and Princess of Wales is an odious exhibition of journalists dabbling their fingers in the stuff of other people's souls.'

Meanwhile, newspapers run stories under headlines such as CHARLES MAY NEVER BE KING.

• **August:** The *Sun* splashes extracts from the so-called 'Squidgy' tapes across ten pages and provides a phone line for readers to listen to them (60,000 people ring the number at 36p a minute). They hear a 30-minute tapped telephone conversation in which James Gilbey, heir to his family's gin fortune, refers to Diana as 'Squidge' and Squidgy'. She complains of feeling confined, and describes her treatment as 'real torture'.

A REGENCY RAKE

The intrigues, animosities and sexually explicit revelations which engulfed the royal circle during the Charles/Diana years were reminiscent of the bitter battles between the Prince Regent (later George IV) and his wife, Caroline of Brunswick.

- Like Charles, 'Prinnie' had a long-time lover, Maria Fitzherbert. Like Charles, he very soon lost any affection for his new wife, and there was open warfare between them. And, like Charles, he found himself much less popular with the British people than the woman he drove to despair.

- George (unlike Charles) turned up drunk to his wedding, and complained that his bride talked too much and was smelly. She told courtiers that he was 'very fat and nothing like as handsome as his portrait'.

- The prince's supporters spread the rumour that Caroline had taken lovers and had an illegitimate child – a claim investigated by the prime minister and three other leading politicians, and found to be false.

- Caroline eventually went home to Germany (and who could blame her?), but when George inherited the throne she returned to England hoping to take up her position as Queen. George had attempted to have the marriage dissolved, but there had been 800 petitions in Caroline's favour, attracting nearly a million signatures. 'I shall support her as long as I can,' the novelist Jane Austen wrote to a friend, 'because she is a woman and because I hate her husband.'

• The most dramatic confrontation occurred at Westminister Abbey in July 1821, when George was crowned King. He had banned Caroline from the Coronation ceremony, but she turned up anyway and tried to force her way inside. Bayonets were held under her chin and the door was slammed in her face.

• As with Charles and Diana, all these dramas were played out in full public view. There was no television, of course, but this was a golden age for cartoonists such as Gillray and the Cruikshanks, and they mercilessly lampooned the overweight and self-indulgent monarch in a vivid gallery of unforgiving illustrations.

• **September:** The *Sun* reveals that Diana had a relationship with James Hewitt, a Household Cavalry officer. The red-headed Hewitt admits the relationship but denies rumours that he is Prince Harry's father: he first met Diana, he says, when the prince was a toddler.

In the same month the TV station ITN runs a documentary about the collapse of the marriage – and the Palace at last admits it.

• **November:** The *Daily Mirror* reveals the existence of a 'Camillagate' tape – another illictly recorded telephone conversation, this time containing intimate exchanges between Charles and his mistress. It quotes Charles saying 'I love you . . . I adore you,' but further extracts appear only the following January in the *Sun* and *Today* newspapers.

For the most part these are commonplace lovers' banalities, but at one point the expressions of longing become quite excruciating. Their farewells take an age, neither wanting to put the phone down.

CHARITABLE CHARLES

In recording the prince's more embarrassing moments, we should also give credit where it's due – he does great, and varied, work for charity.

Apart from being president of a group of not-for-profit organisations under the umbrella of The Prince's Charities, he is the founder and prime mover of The Prince's Trust, which works with 14- to 30-year-olds who have struggled at school, have been in care, are long-term unemployed or have been in trouble with the law. More than 600,000 of them have been helped since the Trust was formed in 1976.

• **December:** The royal family's press secretary calls the tabloids 'a cancer in the soft underbelly of the nation', but after the Queen's Christmas message refers to 'some difficult days this year', *The Times* pronounces: 'What matters is the national sense that something is wrong with the state of the royal family, that, while the monarch remains high in her subjects' esteem, the rest of "the firm" is variously at fault and failing to live and work as it should.'

MEA CULPA

All that remained now was for the two protagonists to complete their public humiliation by volunteering to appear in the 'confessional' of the television studios.

Charles was first out of the blocks. In June 1994 he agreed to be take part in a two-and-a-half hour ITV documentary on his life, with his biographer, Jonathan Dimbleby, as the interviewer. He had been advised by his private secretary Commander Richard Aylard to face up to questions about his adultery, and the poor chap lost his job when the prince's frankness caused an uproar. Some three-quarters of the way through, he was asked whether he had tried to be 'faithful and honourable' when he married:

Charles: 'Yes, absolutely.'

Dimbleby: 'And you were?'

Charles: 'Yes. Until it became irretrievably broken down, us both having tried.'

This admission brought screaming headlines, but it seems not to have bothered the prince himself very much, because he later congratulated Dimbleby on his 'extraordinary ability to listen while I tried to answer your appalling questions'.

QUEEN OF HEARTS

Diana's turn came in November the following year. Her hour-long, emotionally charged interview with Martin Bashir on the BBC's *Panorama* programme would, a decade later, be voted by viewers as the best-remembered programme of all time.

She spoke bitterly about her treatment by 'the establishment I moved into'.

- She had suffered postnatal depression after the birth of William: 'It gave everybody a new label – Diana's unstable and Diana's mentally unbalanced.'

- She had also suffered from bulimia for a number of years: 'It was a symptom of what was going on in my marriage.'

- Finding little support in her taxing public role, she had harmed herself, and Charles hadn't understood: 'But then, not many people would have taken the time to see that.'

- On Camilla: 'There were three of us in this marriage, so it was a bit crowded.'

- Charles hadn't allowed her to have any interests of her own: 'I think that I've always been the 18-year-old girl he got engaged to.'

- She admitted to adultery with James Hewitt, who later wrote a book which she felt betrayed her: 'I adored him. Yes, I was in love with him, but I was very let down.'

- On whether Charles should be king: 'Because I know the character I would think that the top job, as I call it, would bring enormous limitations to him, and I don't know whether he could adapt to that.'

- On the role of the royals: 'I would like a monarchy that has more contact with its people – and I don't mean by riding round on bicycles and things like that, but just having a more in-depth understanding.'

- On her public role and her charity work: 'I'd like to be a queen of people's hearts, but I don't see myself being Queen of this country.'

BYE BYE, *BRITANNIA*

Nothing symbolised the monarchy's decline from grandeur more starkly than the decommissioning of the Royal Yacht *Britannia* in 1997 and the decision not to replace her.

Since bringing the Queen and Prince Philip home from that first Commonwealth tour in 1953 (see page 60), she had carried the royal family on almost a thousand official voyages, from the South Seas to Antarctica, travelling more than a million nautical miles (around 2 million km) and calling in at 600 ports in 135 countries. She is now a tourist attraction in the historic port of Leith, Edinburgh.

ENOUGH IS ENOUGH

All this hearts-on-sleeves stuff from the wretchedly unhappy couple finally became too much for the real Queen to bear.

'After considering the present situation,' a spokesman said in December 1995, 'the Queen wrote to both the prince and princess earlier this week and gave them her view, supported by the Duke of Edinburgh, that an early divorce is desirable.'

She had her way the following August, after which Diana was stripped of her 'Royal Highness' tag but received a lump sum settlement of around £17 million, continued to be known as the Princess of Wales, and retained her apartment at Kensington Palace.

But the Queen's greatest test in this grim period of her reign was to present itself, in all its horror, on the last day of August 1997 – and it was a test that, at first, she was judged to have failed.

A NATION IN MOURNING

In the early hours of that Sunday morning, Diana and her partner Dodi Fayed were killed when their Mercedes crashed in a Paris subway. She died, as she had lived, pursued by paparazzi (on motorcycles, chasing her car) and her last moments, as so many in her very public life, brought sensational headlines.

An autopsy revealed that their driver, Henri Paul, had been more than three times over the alcohol limit, and had taken drugs too, while Dodi's father – Harrod's owner Mohamed Al-Fayed – made lurid accusations about the invovement of the secret services and the House of Windsor in her death.

Back in Britain there were scenes of mourning so tumultuous that they caught every observer by surprise. It was no secret that Diana had been popular – much more so than her former husband – but her death evoked a spontaneous and very 'un-British' outpouring of grief, with people flocking into London in their tens of thousands to pay their respects.

A line of floral tributes soon stretched for half a mile outside Kensington Palace, and fields of flowers adorned the entrances to Buckingham Palace and St James's Palace. There were eventually more than a million of them.

And then there came the anger:

- Why had the royal family – on holiday in Balmoral – said absolutely nothing as the sad hours dragged by? (Because the Queen was preparing a considered response.)

GOODBYE, ENGLAND'S ROSE

At the funeral Elton John sang a reworked version of 'Candle in the Wind', which he had written with Bernie Taupin in 1973 in memory of Marilyn Monroe.

The new version for Diana was entitled 'Goodbye, England's Rose', and the sugar-coated lyrics expressed the tearful sentiments of the moment:

> Loveliness we've lost,
> These empty days without your smile.
> This torch we'll always carry
> For our nation's golden child.

- Why didn't they come straight back to London? (Because they were comforting Diana's sons.)

- Why wasn't the Union flag being flown at half-mast above Buckingham Palace, as it was on so many public buildings in the capital? (Because protocol ruled that the flag was raised only when the monarch was in residence.)

Protocol notwithstanding, Prime Minister Tony Blair had his finger much more sensitively applied to the national pulse. Having immediately dubbed Diana 'The People's Princess' – he was good at soundbites – he now desperately worked the phones in an attempt to save the monarchy's tattered reputation. That flag was eventually flown at half-mast, and the Queen, now back in London, came out of the Palace with Prince Philip to inspect the flowers and read the heartfelt messages people had attached to them.

When, on the day of the funeral, Diana's coffin passed by on its way to Westminster Abbey, the Queen bowed her head towards it.

KEEPING UP THE GOOD WORK

In September 1997 the Diana, Princess of Wales Memorial Fund was established to continue her humanitarian work at home and overseas. Its four chief goals are:

• To ensure palliative care is integrated into the care and treatment of people with HIV/AIDS, cancer and other life-limiting illnesses in sub-Saharan Africa.

• To ensure that refugees and people seeking asylum in the UK are treated with fairness, humanity and in accordance with international law.

• To promote fair treatment and better futures for the most vulnerable people in the criminal justice system.

• To promote the protection of civilians during and after conflict by bringing an end to the use of cluster munitions in warfare.

A BROTHER'S REVENGE

The Queen's gesture could not spare her a coded, but wincingly strong, assault on the royals by Diana's brother, Charles Spencer, in his speech at the Abbey. His sister, he pointedly remarked to an audience of millions around the world, 'needed no royal title to continue to generate her particular brand of magic'.

Attacking the tabloid papers (which he had banned from the service), he in effect pointed the finger at the Palace for failing to give his sister proper protection from them – and promised her sons that the Spencers would do what the Windsors had failed to do:

'She would want us today to pledge ourselves to protecting her beloved boys William and Harry from a similar fate, and I do this here, Diana, on your behalf. We will not allow them to suffer the anguish that used regularly to drive you to tearful despair.

'And beyond that, on behalf of your mother and sisters, I pledge that we, your blood family, will do all we can to continue the imaginative way in which you were steering these two exceptional young men so that their souls are not simply immersed by duty and tradition but can sing openly as you planned.'

Applause, shockingly, broke out both in the Abbey and among the thousands listening to the service outside, for Spencer's barb both reflected the mood of the times and reinforced it. The Windsors, he implied, were dull, unfeeling and hidebound. The fairytale princess had gone, leaving behind a court of cardboard royal cut-outs.

IN MEMORIAM

Remembering Diana became something of an obsession in the months and years after her death, from the relatively grand (the memorial fountain in Hyde Park) to the ephemeral (the canna lily 'Princess Di' and at least three rose hybrids were named after her).

She was honoured abroad, too. A 'Diana memorial garden' was created in Cuba, and Russian scientists who discovered a new light blue rock in Siberia decided to call it 'dianite'.

TOO LITTLE, TOO LATE

Three days later the Queen at last paid tribute to 'an exceptional and gifted human being'. No-one who knew Diana, she said, would ever forget her.

'Millions of others who never met her, but felt they knew her, will remember her. I for one believe that there are lessons to be drawn from her life and from the extraordinary and moving reaction to her death. I share in your determination to cherish her memory.'

However sincerely meant, it had come too late. As a battered and bruised monarchy limped towards the millennium's finishing line, and Elizabeth towards her fiftieth year on the throne, the royal family was seen to be out of synch with the mood of the times.

It needed a new shot in the arm . . .

'NOUGHTIES' BRITAIN

2000 Millennium Dome, Millennium Bridge and Tate Modern art gallery open; Hatfield rail crash.

2001 Foot and mouth epidemic; Eden Project opens; Selby rail crash; 67 British nationals killed in 9/11 terrorist attacks on US.

2002 Potters Bar rail crash; Soham murders.

2003 Protests against Iraq war; London congestion charge introduced; Hutton Inquiry into death of Dr David Kelly.

2004 27 Chinese cockle pickers drowned in Morecambe Bay; foxhunting banned.

2005 Tube and bus terrorist attacks in London; pubs allowed to stay open for 24 hours.

2006 Russian dissident Alexander Litvinenko poisoned by Polonium-210 in London; five prostitutes murdered in Ipswich.

2007 New Wembley Stadium opens; smoking ban in enclosed public spaces.

2008 World banking crisis; Northern Rock bank nationalised; Heathrow airport's Terminal 5 opens.

2009 First recession since 1991; swine flu outbreak; MPs' expenses controversy.

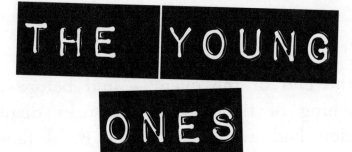

How did Victoria celebrate her Golden Jubilee in 1887? By staging a banquet at Buckingham Palace for 50 kings and princes, plus the heads of Britain's overseas colonies and dominions.

And Elizabeth in 2002? With an exuberant 'Party at the Palace' bringing together possibly the most stellar gathering of rock and pop musicians ever to strut a shared stage, with Brian May (formerly of Queen) performing 'God Save the Queen' as a guitar solo on the roof.

THE SON AND HEIR

At the end of the event – and before the launching of the largest fireworks display London had even seen – the royal family joined the stars on stage, with Prince Charles thanking his mother for her 50 years at the helm. 'Your majesty,' he began . . . 'Mummy!'

It was, in its combination of the personal with the quaintly upper-class usage, an address neatly poised between two registers. The royals were almost as down-to-earth as the rest of us – but still not quite.

But that was Charles in a nutshell. You could sympathise with his boyhood suffering at Gordonstoun school ('Colditz in kilts,' he called it), an experience which perhaps reinforced the softer, more reflective side of his nature – talking to plants, for instance – while recoiling from the more blimpish of his public pronouncements about art and architecture.

You could shake your head at his treatment of Diana while admiring his devotion to a wide range of good causes. You might be touched by his pleasure in the anarchic humour of the Goons, yet be frustrated by his stubborn addiction to a pampered, ceremonial way of life which surely belonged to yesterday.

SAYING SORRY

When Charles married Camilla in April 2005 (she became HRH the Duchess of Cornwall) he was the first member of the royal family ever to be wed in a civil ceremony.

The service was conducted at the Guildhall, Windsor, by the Archbishop of Canterbury, and the couple read an act of penitence from the 1662 *Book of Common Prayer:*

'We acknowledge and bewail our manifold sins and wickedness, which we, from time to time, most grievously have committed, by thought, word and deed, against thy Divine Majesty, provoking most justly thy wrath and indignation against us.'

PALACE NAUGHTIES

Perhaps there would never again be the maelstrom of torrid revelations that accompanied the Charles/Diana rift, but the royals weren't spared further awkward media moments during the 'noughties'.

2000 Diana's former senior aide Patrick Jephson writes the memoir *Shadows of a Princess*, and is accused by Prince William of betraying his mother's trust.

2002 Diana's 'rock', her butler Paul Burrell, is accused of stealing hundreds of her personal belongings, but the case collapses after the Queen suddenly remembers that Diana had given him permission to look after them.

2003 Burrell publishes his best-selling *A Royal Duty*, which tells of his life with Diana – and covers the aborted court case.

'Comedy terrorist' Aaron Barschak gate-crashes Prince William's 21st birthday party, wearing a pink dress, a false beard and a turban, prompting an investigation into security at Windsor Castle.

2005 The *Mail on Sunday* publishes extracts from Prince Charles's 1997 diary, in which he describes the handing over of Hong Kong as 'the great

Chinese takeaway' and the Chinese leaders as 'appalling old waxworks'. He wins an injunction against the newspaper.

2006 Prince Harry apologises after the *Sun* prints pictures of him wearing a swastika armband to a friend's fancy-dress party.

2007 The *News of the World*'s royal editor, Clive Goodman, and a private investigator, Glenn Mulcaire, are jailed for tapping the phones of three royals.

After Prince Harry is presented with his pilot's 'wings', the al-Qaeda terrorist group threatens to abduct him if he flies an Apache attack helicopter in Afghanistan.

2009 Prince Harry apologises for using the word 'Paki' to refer to a member of his platoon while filming a video diary. (The film was made in 2006 but is only now reported in the press.) As his camera pans across a group of other cadets at a training camp he asks, 'Anybody else around here? Ah, our little Paki friend, Ahmed.'

2012 Prince Harry courts controversy again when he's photographed naked with an unknown young woman during a game of strip billiards in a Las Vegas hotel room.

THE NEXT GENERATION

If Charles's shame and ridicule at the hands of the media were still etched in the public memory in the early years of the new millennium, suggestions that he might one day decline the crown seemed wide of the mark. The Queen Mother had died early in the Jubilee year at the age of 101, and if the Queen were to sail into old age as confidently, Charles would be around 80 before he came to the throne. Who knew what his reputation would be then?

All royalist eyes were now turning to the young princes, William and Harry. True, William himself might be well into his sixties before becoming king, but the wearing of the crown wasn't the issue for those who wished the monarchy well. More important was the creation of an image which resonated well with the public at large.

'The monarchy is finished. It was finished a while ago, but they're still making the corpses dance.'
Novelist and playwright Sue Townsend

TICKING THE BOXES

Their grandmother had given the institution a boost with her Golden Jubilee celebrations in 2002 (a four-day affair, with beacons lit across the country). A survey by the MORI polling institute revealed that she had just scored her highest popularity ratings in two decades.

- Some 82 per cent of Britons said they were satisfied with the Queen, and 80 per cent supported the monarchy in general.

- The Jubilee celebrations were enjoyed by 77 per cent of the population.

- Asked whether the Queen should retire at a certain age, 25 per cent thought she should step down at 80 (in 2006), while 69 per cent thought she should go on for as long as she was able.

- Asked what should follow if the Queen retired, 47 per cent said the monarchy should be left as it was; 35 per cent preferred a scaled-down version of the monarchy, with a lesser role and fewer members; and 17 per cent wanted an elected head of state.

THE MONARCHY – YES OR NO?

For	Against
The monarchy reflects tradition and national identity.	Its quaint practices are completely at odds with life in modern Britain.
The Queen stands above politics.	Her position enshrines ancient class divides.
Her political role is symbolic and poses no threat to democracy.	The symbolism insults and infantilises her 'loyal subjects'.
She frees the prime minister from ceremonial duties.	Other heads of state have no problem fulfilling both roles.
The trappings of royalty attract large revenues from tourism.	The cost of the monarchy to the nation is disproportionate.
The Queen and her family work tirelessly for charity.	Their great wealth would allow that to continue privately.
The Queen is highly respected by the nation and all over the world.	True, but the monarchy is hereditary. Who comes next?

- Asked how long the British monarchy would survive, 82 per cent forecast that it would be around for another ten years; 41 per cent gave it 50 years; and only 24 per cent believed it would still exist in 100 years' time.

- As for Charles, 52 per cent thought he would make a good king and 28 per cent a bad one.

BOYS NEXT DOOR

This is where the fixation on the younger generation comes in. It's all very well for the monarchy to be on Facebook and Twitter (don't expect a personal reply), but William and Harry were the first royals to look as if they might make a fist of sharing a relaxed pint with strangers in the pub.

This supposed ordinariness is apt to be over-egged (their upbringing and home life have been rather different from ours, after all), and yet – not all diehard royalists would approve – they do seem to fit the society around them to a far greater extent than their father, let alone their grandmother. Perhaps, as their uncle hoped, they will follow their mother's lead and learn to 'sing'.

A PEOPLE'S WEDDING

William met Kate Middleton while they were both studying the history of art at St Andrews University in Scotland, and they married several years later, in April 2011. ('They've been practising long enough,' Charles commented rather indecorously.) Gone was the demand that a royal bride, and future queen, should come from a high-born family: her parents met when they were both cabin crew for an airline, and they later set up an online children's partyware business.

Although the ceremony was held in Westminster Abbey, the guest list included friends from days gone by as well as children, volunteers and the homeless in what the groom decided should be a unique 'people's royal wedding' – with echoes of Diana. (Fergie, notably, was *not* invited, having been involved in at least one scandal too many.)

And where would the happy couple live once the festivities were over? In a £750-a-month Welsh cottage (albeit with stunning views of Snowdonia and access to a private beach), while the Prince undertook a three-year search-and-rescue pilot's posting at RAF Valley. They would have no live-in servants – although unfortunately William would need a 15-strong armed security team and Kate a guard of her own, too. Restyled Catherine for official duties, she would doubtless throw herself into a life of charity work.

And so the nation indulged itself in one of its periodic royal junkettings. The day (a Friday) was declared a Bank Holiday, which meant that the nation could enjoy back-to-back four-day weekends over the Easter period – with not a few revellers allowing themselves a full 11-day 'Wills and Kate' wedding break.

Not everyone was delighted. The Cumbrian artist Lydia Leith created a royal wedding sick bag, with the slogan 'Throne up'. But 5,500 roads were closed for street parties, and police estimated that in London a million people lined the route of the wedding procession.

For once the Queen could happily take a back seat. After all, it was a kind of dress rehearsal for another massive party of her own . . .

ALL THIS AND THE OLYMPICS, TOO!

In July 2005 London beat Paris 54–50 in a nail-biting vote for the honour of staging the Olympics seven years later – and so guaranteed the capital a momentous, and tourist-packed, summer.

'We're taking home the biggest prize in sport,' rejoiced Lord Coe, the chairman of the organising committee.

The long weekend of 2–5 June 2012 was earmarked for the Queen's Diamond Jubilee celebrations, with the Olympics following between 27 July and 12 August.

Some Londoners unmoved by sport or royalty vowed to travel abroad to avoid both the crush and the hype, while others criticised the vast expenditure on the two events. For many, though, they offered a welcome distraction during the gloom of an economic recession.

'The Queen has been an outstanding head of state. It is important that the Diamond Jubilee is not drowned out by the Olympics.'
–Andrew Rosindell MP

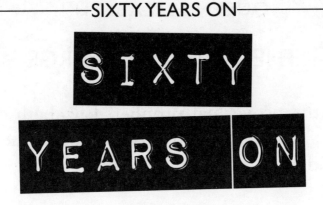

The young princess who came down from her treetop hideaway to claim the throne in 1952 (see pages 18–19) can never have imagined the manifold trials and tribulations that would beset her reign over the ensuing 60 years, and yet her much older, infinitely more experienced self surely woke on the dawn of her Diamond Jubilee with all the satisfaction of a battle-worn survivor. After all, although the monarchy's blue-chip stock had taken a tumble on the index of public opinion, 'the firm' was still in business – and that hadn't always seemed inevitable.

THE WORLD AT LARGE

Like the proverbial prophet, Elizabeth could reflect that she was probably more honoured abroad than in her own country.

Back in 1952 Britain was already a declining power on the world stage, but 60 years on she could still enjoy the esteem of ruling over a significant clutch of Commonwealth countries around the globe.

AN EXCLUSIVE CLUB

At the time of the Diamond Jubilee Britain was one of 44 nations in the world having a monarch as head of state. The Queen led the way, heading 16 Commonwealth realms which recognised her as their head of state.

By 2015 the historical form of absolute monarchy was retained only in Brunei, Oman, Qatar, Saudi Arabia, Swaziland and the United Arab Emirates – plus Vatican City, over which the Pope, though elected by the cardinals, has complete legislative, executive and judicial powers.

There had even been an unexpected triumph in November 1999, when the country most likely to go its own republican way and renounce its allegiance to the Crown – Australia – opted for the status quo. (The referendum attracted a 95 per cent turn-out, with 55 per cent in favour of the monarchy.)

MONEY MATTERS

Financially there had been significant changes over the six decades, with power shifting decisively from the royal family to the government. Not only was the Queen now paying income tax, but in 2010 it was revealed that the Palace had been forced to give up the right to manage the royal finances: the government was to have the final say in how she could spend the £38 million given to her by Parliament every year.

By the Jubilee year, it now appeared, the royal household would be broke unless it agreed to substantial savings – with the Queen running down the reserves in order to fulfil her duties. A cash-flow crisis had forced officials to cut down on every aspect of her expenditure, including staff, uniforms, stationery and soft furnishings.

'The royal household is acutely aware of the difficult economic climate,' announced the Keeper of the Privy Purse, Sir Alan Reid. 'We are implementing a headcount freeze and reviewing every vacancy to see if we can avoid replacement.'

For the record, here's a run-down of Palace spending for 2009–2010:

• Garden parties £700,000
• Food and kitchens £500,000
• Recruitment and training £300,000
• Stationery £300,000
• Legal advice £200,000
• Computers and IT £200,000
• Housekeeping £300,000
• Furnishings £300,000
• Carriage processions £100,000
• Uniforms and protective clothing £100,000
• Cars and other vehicles £100,000.

The Queen's private wealth was another matter, but the monarchy had tightened its belt.

OFF WITH HER HEAD?

The monarch's head has appeared on postage stamps ever since the 'penny black' went on sale in 1840, but in 2010 draft government legislation to sell Royal Mail – possibly to a foreign buyer – included no guarantee that the tradition would be upheld.

After a media outcry, and discussions between politicians and Buckingham Palace, the parliamentary bill was amended the following January so that any purchaser would be required to include an image of the Queen.

BY ROYAL APPOINTMENT

More than 800 companies and individuals hold royal warrants for supplying the Queen, Prince Philip or Prince Charles for at least five consecutive years. In 2011, however, the decision by leading brands such as After Eight mint chocolates and Jacob's Cream Crackers not to display the 'by appointment' legend led to suggestions that the honour had lost some of its significance in a less deferential age.

Mohamed al-Fayed at Harrod's (see page 157) went further in his anger against the royal family over the crash which killed Diana and his son. In 2009 he had the store's four warrants removed – and burnt.

UNDERLINGS

Despite all the economies, however, the flunkeys and fripperies had by no means gone away in the harsher world of 2012. Few of the royals were now paid from the public purse, but the Queen herself could still count on a good measure of the traditional bowing and scraping.

On formal occasions she was, as ever, protected by her bodyguards, Gold Stick-in-Waiting or his deputy, Silver Stick-in-Waiting, while at the State Opening of Parliament she would find her Lord Chancellor reassuringly decked out in his fancy Gilbert & Sullivan attire as he gingerly backed away from her majestic presence.

At home, her Palace was inhabited by countless underlings in the way of stewards, equerries, mistresses of the robes, maids of honour and ladies of the bedchamber, so ensuring that she never had to lift a finger.

COUNTING ONE'S BLESSINGS

And then there was the good luck of her health. Queen Victoria, the only other English monarch to clock up 60 years in the job, had celebrated her diamond jubilee on the steps of St Paul's because her 78-year-old legs couldn't make it to the top. Elizabeth, at 86, was still spry and seemingly set fair for her platinum occasion another ten years on.

Indeed, as she set off from the Palace on her grand Jubilee procession she could surely be forgiven a little smugness. So much had changed in her public and private worlds since the innocent days of 1952, and yet here she was, unbowed, about to bestow the royal wave on another adoring, flag-waving crowd.

That fabulous golden coach had trundled over many a rocky road down the years, but – triumphantly – it still had its wheels on!

GLOSSARY

Bank Holiday A public holiday in the UK.

bulimia A disorder in which bouts of over-eating are followed by self-induced purging.

cargo cult A belief system whose adherents expect the arrival of ancestral spirits bearing gifts.

firm, the A nickname for the royal family, apparently used by the royals themselves.

Fleet Street Britain's national newspapers (formerly based in this London street).

ghillie A Scottish gamekeeper or rural servant.

HRH His/Her Royal Highness – a title held by some members of the royal family.

IRA Irish Republican Army, a militant group advocating home rule for all of Ireland.

mad cow disease A nickname for bovine spongiform encephalopathy (BSE), a cattle disease that may be transmitted to humans.

MEP Member of the European Parliament.

Mods and Rockers Gangs of young people who clashed on British streets in the 1960s.

VAT Value-added tax.

Yeomen of the Guard The Queen's ceremonial bodyguards.

TIMELINE

1926 Elizabeth born, 26 April.

1940 Princess Elizabeth, 14, makes her first public broadcast.

1947 Elizabeth marries Philip Mountbatten.

1948 Prince Charles born.

1950 Princess Anne born.

1952 Elizabeth ascends the throne on the death of her father, George VI.

1953 Coronation. Hillary and Tenzing climb Everest. Queen and Philip begin six-month Commonwealth tour. Launch of Royal Yacht *Britannia*.

1960 Prince Andrew born.

1964 Prince Edward born.

1969 Prince Charles invested as Prince of Wales. Film *Royal Family* shown.

1970 First royal walkabout, in Australia.

1974 Princess Anne survives kidnap attempt.

1977 Silver Jubilee celebrations. Virginia Wade wins Wimbledon.

1978 Princess Margaret and Lord Snowdon divorce.

1981 Prince Charles marries Lady Diana Spencer. Marcus Serjeant fires at the Queen during Trooping the Colour.

1982 Michael Fagan breaks into the Queen's bedroom at Buckingham Palace.

1987 Prince Edward produces TV programme *It's a Royal Knockout*.

1988 Prince Charles narrowly avoids death on the ski slopes at Klosters.

1992 The *Annus Horribilis*. Divorce of Princess Anne and Mark Phillips. Separation of the prince and princess of Wales and the duke and duchess of York. Publication of Andrew Morton's *Diana: Her True Story*. *Sun* newspaper publishes extracts from the 'Squidgy' tapes. Windsor Castle is badly damaged by fire. *Sun* leaks the Queen's Christmas Day speech.

1993 Queen and Prince Charles agree to pay income tax. *Daily Mirror* reporter infiltrates Buckingham Palace and Windsor Castle. Buckingham Palace opens to the public.

1994 Charles admits adultery in TV documentary.

1995 Diana's 'Queen of Hearts' TV interview. Queen urges Charles and Diana to divorce.

1996 Divorce of prince and princess of Wales and duke and duchess of York.

1997 Diana killed in car crash. Royal Yacht *Britannia* decommissioned.

1999 Prince Edward marries Sophie Rhys-Jones. Footman demoted for giving alcohol to the Queen's corgis.

2000 Patrick Jephson publishes *Shadows of a Princess*.

2002 Deaths of Princess Margaret and the Queen

Mother. Elizabeth II's Golden Jubilee. Paul Burrell is accused of stealing Diana's property, but the case collapses.

2003 Burrell publishes *A Royal Duty*. Aaron Barschak gatecrashes Prince William's birthday party at Windsor.

2005 Prince Charles marries Camilla Parker Bowles.

2006 Prince Harry apologises for wearing swastika fancy dress.

2007 Elizabeth becomes Britain's oldest reigning monarch.

2009 Prince Harry apologises for calling a member of his platoon a 'Paki'.

2010 Queen's first great-grandchild, Savannah, born to Peter Phillips (son of Princess Anne) and his wife Autumn.

2011 Prince William marries Catherine (Kate) Middleton. Queen makes first royal visit to Ireland since independence.

2012 Queen's Diamond Jubilee.

2013 The birth of Prince George of Cambridge, the son of Prince William, Duke of Cambridge, and Catherine, Duchess of Cambridge.

2015 The birth of Princess Charlotte of Cambridge, the daughter of the Duke and Duchess of Cambridge.

INDEX

Very Peculiar Histories™
at The Cherished Library

History of the British Isles
England (in 3 volumes)
  Vol. 1: From Ancient Times to Agincourt
    David Arscott   978-1-908973-37-5
  Vol. 2: From the Wars of the Roses to the
    Industrial Revolution *Ian Graham*   978-1-908973-38-2
  Vol. 3: From Trafalgar to the New Elizabethans
    John Malam   978-1-908973-39-9
Scotland (in 2 volumes) *Fiona Macdonald*
  Vol. 1: From Ancient Times to Robert the Bruce
                                             978-1-906370-91-6
  Vol. 2: From the Stewarts to Modern Scotland
                                             978-1-906714-79-6

  Boxed set of both Scottish volumes: 978-1-909645-03-5
Ireland *Jim Pipe*   978-1-905638-98-7
Wales *Rupert Matthews*   978-1-907184-19-2

History of the 20th century
Titanic *Jim Pipe*   978-1-907184-87-1
World War One *Jim Pipe*   978-1-908177-00-1
World War Two *Jim Pipe*   978-1-908177-97-1
The Blitz *David Arscott*   978-1-907184-18-5
Rations *David Arscott*   978-1-907184-25-3
Make Do and Mend *Jacqueline Morley*   978-1-910184-45-5

Social history
Victorian Servants *Fiona Macdonald*   978-1-907184-49-9
Wine *David Arscott*   978-1-910184-88-2

North of the Border
Dundee *Fiona Macdonald*   978-1-910184-01-1
Edinburgh *Fiona Macdonald*   978-1-908973-82-5
Great Scots *Fiona Macdonald*   978-1-909645-20-2
Scottish Clans *Fiona Macdonald*   978-1-908759-90-0
Scottish Tartan and Highland Dress
  Fiona Macdonald   978-1-908759-89-4
Scottish Words *Fiona Macdonald*   978-1-908759-63-4
Whisky *Fiona Macdonald*   978-1-907184-76-5

Folklore and traditions
Christmas *Fiona Macdonald*   978-1-907184-50-5

British places
Brighton *David Arscott*   978-1-906714-89-5
Dundee *Fiona Macdonald*   978-1-910184-01-1
Edinburgh *Fiona Macdonald*   978-1-908973-82-5
London *Jim Pipe*   978-1-907184-26-0
Oxford *David Arscott*   978-1-908973-81-8
Yorkshire *John Malam*   978-1-907184-57-4

Famous Britons
Great Britons *Ian Graham*   978-1-907184-59-8
Great Scots *Fiona Macdonald*   978-1-909645-20-2
Robert Burns *Fiona Macdonald*   978-1-908177-71-1
Charles Dickens *Fiona Macdonald*   978-1-908177-15-5
William Shakespeare *Jacqueline Morley*   978-1-908177-14-8

Sports and pastimes
Cricket *Jim Pipe*   978-1-908177-90-2
Fishing *Rob Beattie*   978-1-908177-91-9
Golf *David Arscott*   978-1-907184-75-8
The World Cup *David Arscott*   978-1-909645-21-9

Royalty
Kings & Queens of Great Britain
  Antony Mason   978-1-906714-77-2
The Tudors *Jim Pipe*   978-1-907184-58-1

Natural history
Cats *Fiona Macdonald*   978-1-908973-34-4
Dogs *Fiona Macdonald*   978-1-908973-35-1
Gardening *Jacqueline Morley*   978-1-909645-19-6

Ancient and medieval history
Ancient Egyptian Mummies *Jim Pipe*   978-1-909645-08-0
Castles *Jacqueline Morley*   978-1-907184-48-2